I0503916

Table Of Contents

Contents

The Wealth mindset

The Wealth mindset

The Wealth mindset

The Wealth mindset

The Wealth mindset

Part 1

The Power of a Wealth Mindset

You will learn about the benefits of adopting a wealth mindset and how it can help you achieve your financial goals. This part will provide real-life examples of individuals who have transformed their lives through mindset shifts and explain how readers can do the same.

Chapter 1

1.1 What is a Wealth Mindset?

A wealth mindset is a way of thinking and behaving that emphasizes the pursuit of financial abundance and success. It is based on a set of beliefs, attitudes, and habits that enable individuals to create and maintain wealth over time. The wealth mindset emphasizes the importance of taking proactive steps towards financial success, such as saving, investing, and actively seeking out opportunities for growth.

At the core of a wealth mindset is a belief in the attainability of wealth. Individuals with this mindset believe that they can achieve financial success through hard work and smart financial decisions. They understand that creating wealth is a process that takes time, effort, and strategy, but they also believe that success is within reach for those who are willing to put in the effort.

One important aspect of the wealth mindset is a willingness to take calculated risks. Individuals with this mindset are not afraid to step outside their comfort zone and pursue opportunities that have the potential to yield significant returns. They understand that taking risks is an essential part of building wealth and are willing to accept the possibility of failure as a necessary part of the process. However, they also carefully evaluate risks before taking them and work to minimize potential losses.

Another key aspect of the wealth mindset is a commitment to ongoing learning and personal development. Individuals with this mindset recognize that there is always more to learn about finance, investing, and wealth-building. They seek out information and resources that can help them improve their financial knowledge and skills, and are open to new ideas and strategies that can help them achieve their financial goals. They also understand the importance of adapting to changes in the financial landscape and staying informed about market trends.

Individuals with a wealth mindset also tend to be proactive and focused on their goals. They have a clear vision of what they want to achieve financially, and are willing to take the necessary steps to make that vision a reality. They are able to prioritize their time and resources effectively, and are not easily distracted by short-term setbacks or obstacles. They also understand that setbacks are a normal part of the wealth-building process and are able to stay motivated and persistent in the face of challenges.

Another key aspect of a wealth mindset is the ability to manage emotions related to money. Wealth can be a powerful motivator, but it can also be a source of anxiety, stress, and even guilt. Individuals with a wealth mindset are able to manage these emotions and maintain a healthy relationship with money. They understand that money is just a tool and that their self-worth is not defined by their net worth. They also have a sense of perspective and balance in their financial lives, recognizing the importance of financial security but also the value of experiences, relationships, and personal growth.

In addition to managing emotions related to money, individuals with a wealth mindset also tend to have a positive attitude towards risk. They recognize that there are no guarantees when it comes to investing or entrepreneurship, but they are willing to take calculated risks in order to achieve their goals. They are also able to learn from their mistakes and use setbacks as opportunities for growth and improvement.

In these core characteristics, a wealth mindset is also marked by specific beliefs and habits related to money management and wealth-building. For example, individuals with this mindset tend to view money as a tool for achieving their goals and living a fulfilling life, rather than an end in itself. They understand the importance of living within their means and avoiding excessive debt. They also prioritize saving and investing for the future, and are willing to make sacrifices in the short-term in order to achieve their long-term financial goals.

Finally, individuals with a wealth mindset tend to have a sense of abundance and gratitude. They recognize the many blessings in their lives, and are able to find joy and fulfillment in the present moment, even as they work towards their future financial goals. They understand that wealth is not just about accumulating money, but also about creating a sense of security, freedom, and fulfillment in life.

In summary, a wealth mindset is a way of thinking and behaving that promotes financial abundance and success. It is characterized by a belief in the attainability of wealth, a willingness to take calculated risks, a commitment to ongoing learning and personal development, a proactive and focused approach to achieving financial goals, specific beliefs and habits related to money management and wealth-building, and a sense of abundance and gratitude. By cultivating a wealth mindset, individuals can increase their chances of achieving financial success and creating a fulfilling and prosperous future for themselves and those around them.

Chapter 2

2.1 The Power of Your Thoughts and Beliefs

The power of your thoughts and beliefs refers to the profound impact that your mindset and mental attitudes can have on your life. In essence, your thoughts and beliefs shape your reality, influencing the way you perceive and interact with the world around you.

The concept of the power of thoughts and beliefs is rooted in the field of positive psychology, which focuses on promoting happiness, well-being, and resilience. Research in this field has demonstrated that individuals who cultivate positive thoughts and beliefs tend to experience greater levels of success, happiness, and overall life satisfaction.

One of the primary ways in which thoughts and beliefs influence our lives is through the process of self-fulfilling prophecies. This refers to the tendency for our beliefs and expectations to shape our behavior and outcomes in a way that confirms those beliefs and expectations.

For example, if you believe that you are not capable of achieving a certain goal, you may not put in the effort required to achieve it, and as a result, you may fail, thus confirming your initial belief. On the other hand, if you believe that you are capable of achieving a goal, you are more likely to put in the effort required to achieve it, and you may experience success, thus reinforcing your initial belief.

Another way in which thoughts and beliefs can impact our lives is through their influence on our emotional and physical health. Negative thoughts and beliefs, such as feelings of hopelessness or helplessness, can lead to chronic stress, anxiety, and depression, which can have a profound impact on our physical health. On the other hand, positive thoughts and beliefs, such as feelings of optimism and gratitude, have been linked to lower levels of stress and better overall health outcomes.

In addition to influencing our behavior and health, thoughts and beliefs can also impact our relationships and social interactions. Our beliefs about ourselves and others can shape the way we approach and engage with others, and can impact the quality of our relationships. For example, individuals who hold negative beliefs about themselves or others may struggle to form meaningful and fulfilling connections, while those with positive beliefs may be more likely to form supportive and nurturing relationships.

So how can we harness the power of our thoughts and beliefs to promote greater happiness, success, and well-being? One key strategy is to cultivate a growth mindset, which refers to the belief that our abilities and intelligence can be developed through effort and hard work. Individuals with a growth mindset tend to be more resilient in the face of setbacks and failures, as they view these as opportunities for growth and improvement rather than evidence of their innate limitations.

It is important to note that our thoughts and beliefs are not fixed, but rather they are malleable and can be shaped and changed through intentional effort and practice. This means that even if you currently hold negative or limiting beliefs about yourself and your abilities, you have the power to transform them into more positive and empowering beliefs.

One effective way to shift your thoughts and beliefs is through cognitive restructuring, which involves identifying and challenging negative or unhelpful thoughts and replacing them with more positive and realistic ones. This process involves paying attention to your internal dialogue and questioning the validity and accuracy of your thoughts and beliefs.

Another important factor to consider when it comes to the power of thoughts and beliefs is the role of socialization and cultural conditioning. Many of our thoughts and beliefs are shaped by the messages we receive from our families, communities, and media, and may not necessarily reflect our own values and beliefs. By becoming aware of these influences, we can begin to challenge and shift our thoughts and beliefs in a more intentional and deliberate way.

In addition to cognitive strategies, there are also behavioral strategies that can help to reinforce positive thoughts and beliefs. For example, setting achievable goals and celebrating small wins can help to build confidence and self-efficacy, which can in turn reinforce positive beliefs about your abilities.

Another important strategy is to practice positive self-talk, which refers to the inner dialogue we have with ourselves. By intentionally cultivating positive thoughts and beliefs about ourselves, we can promote greater self-confidence and resilience, which can in turn improve our ability to cope with challenges and setbacks.

It can be helpful to cultivate a sense of gratitude and appreciation for the blessings in our lives. By focusing on the positive aspects of our lives, we can cultivate a more optimistic and hopeful mindset, which can help us to weather the storms of life with greater grace and resilience.

The power of your thoughts and beliefs refers to the profound impact that your mindset and mental attitudes can have on your life. By cultivating positive thoughts and beliefs, practicing positive self-talk, and cultivating a growth mindset, you can harness this power to promote greater happiness, success, and well-being.

Finally, it is important to recognize that the power of thoughts and beliefs is not a panacea for all of life's challenges. While cultivating positive thoughts and beliefs can certainly improve your overall well-being and success, it is also important to acknowledge that setbacks and failures are an inevitable part of life. By embracing a growth mindset and viewing these challenges as opportunities for learning and growth, you can continue to move forward and achieve your goals, even in the face of adversity.

In summary, the power of thoughts and beliefs is a profound force that can shape our reality and impact our overall well-being and success. By cultivating positive thoughts and beliefs, challenging negative or limiting beliefs, and taking intentional action to reinforce positive beliefs, we can harness this power to achieve greater happiness, resilience, and success in all areas of life.

Chapter 3

3.1 The Benefits of Adopting a Wealth Mindset

Adopting a wealth mindset can have a multitude of benefits for individuals, including improved financial well-being, increased confidence and self-esteem, greater resilience in the face of challenges, and a more positive outlook on life.

One of the primary benefits of adopting a wealth mindset is improved financial well-being. By cultivating a mindset that is focused on abundance and opportunities for growth, individuals are more likely to seek out and capitalize on opportunities to increase their wealth and financial stability. This may involve taking steps such as investing in assets that appreciate over time, pursuing higher-paying career opportunities, or starting a business. By adopting a wealth mindset, individuals can also develop greater financial discipline and make more strategic financial decisions that support their long-term financial goals.

In addition to financial benefits, adopting a wealth mindset can also have a positive impact on one's overall well-being. Individuals with a wealth mindset tend to be more confident and self-assured, as they believe in their ability to create and achieve their own success. This can translate into greater opportunities for personal and professional growth, as individuals with a wealth mindset are more likely to take risks and pursue ambitious goals.

Adopting a wealth mindset can also increase resilience in the face of challenges and setbacks. When individuals believe that they have the power to shape their own reality and create their own success, they are more likely to view obstacles as opportunities for growth and learning, rather than insurmountable barriers. This can help individuals to bounce back more quickly from setbacks and continue to pursue their goals with a sense of optimism and determination.

Another benefit of adopting a wealth mindset is a more positive outlook on life. Individuals with a wealth mindset tend to focus on the abundance of opportunities and resources available to them, rather than dwelling on scarcity or lack. This can lead to greater feelings of gratitude, contentment, and overall life satisfaction.

Adopting a wealth mindset can also have a positive impact on those around us. By modeling a mindset of abundance and success, we can inspire and motivate others to pursue their own goals and achieve greater success in their lives. This can create a ripple effect of positivity and success, leading to greater well-being and prosperity for individuals and communities as a whole.

Adopting a wealth mindset can have a multitude of benefits for individuals, including improved financial well-being, increased confidence and self-esteem, greater resilience in the face of challenges, and a more positive outlook on life. By cultivating a mindset of abundance and focusing on opportunities for growth and success, individuals can achieve greater happiness, prosperity, and fulfillment in all areas of life.

One important aspect of adopting a wealth mindset is developing a sense of abundance and gratitude. This means recognizing and appreciating the abundance of resources and opportunities that exist in the world, rather than focusing on scarcity or lack. When individuals approach life with a sense of abundance, they are more likely to take advantage of opportunities and see potential for growth and success in all areas of their lives.

Another key component of a wealth mindset is a willingness to take calculated risks. This does not mean being reckless or impulsive, but rather being willing to step outside of one's comfort zone and pursue opportunities that may have some degree of uncertainty or risk. By taking calculated risks, individuals can create new opportunities for growth and success that may not have been possible otherwise.

In addition to taking risks, individuals with a wealth mindset also tend to have a strong sense of purpose and direction. They know what they want to achieve and are willing to put in the effort and hard work necessary to achieve their goals. This sense of purpose and direction helps individuals to stay focused and motivated even in the face of setbacks or obstacles.

Finally, adopting a wealth mindset also involves developing a strong sense of personal responsibility and accountability. Rather than blaming external factors for their circumstances, individuals with a wealth mindset take ownership of their lives and recognize that they have the power to shape their own reality. This sense of personal responsibility can be empowering and liberating, as it allows individuals to take control of their lives and create the success and prosperity they desire.

In conclusion, adopting a wealth mindset can have a wide range of benefits for individuals, including improved financial well-being, increased confidence and self-esteem, greater resilience in the face of challenges, and a more positive outlook on life. By cultivating a sense of abundance and gratitude, taking calculated risks, developing a strong sense of purpose and direction, and taking personal responsibility for their lives, individuals can achieve greater success and fulfillment in all areas of their lives.

Chapter 4

4.1 Examples of Successful People with a Wealth Mindset

There are countless examples of successful individuals who have adopted a wealth mindset and achieved great success in their lives. These individuals serve as powerful examples of what is possible when one approaches life with a positive, growth-oriented mindset.

One well-known example is Warren Buffett, one of the world's most successful investors and business leaders. Buffett is known for his long-term perspective and his willingness to invest in undervalued companies with strong fundamentals. He has also been an advocate for simplicity and frugality, living in the same house he purchased in the 1950s and driving a modest car. These habits have allowed him to accumulate a net worth of over $100 billion, making him one of the wealthiest people in the world.

Another example of a successful individual with a wealth mindset is Oprah Winfrey, who rose from a childhood of poverty to become one of the most influential media personalities in the world. Winfrey has been open about the challenges she faced growing up, including poverty, abuse, and discrimination. Despite these challenges, she remained focused on her goals and pursued her passion for media and storytelling. Today, she is worth over $2.7 billion and is widely respected for her philanthropic work and advocacy for social justice.

Elon Musk is another example of an individual with a wealth mindset who has achieved remarkable success. Musk is the founder of SpaceX, Tesla, and other companies that are revolutionizing the fields of space exploration and renewable energy. He is known for his innovative ideas and his willingness to take big risks in pursuit of his goals. Despite facing numerous setbacks and challenges along the way, Musk has remained focused on his vision and has become one of the most influential entrepreneurs of his generation.

Other examples of successful individuals with a wealth mindset include Jeff Bezos, founder of Amazon; Mark Zuckerberg, founder of Facebook; and Richard Branson, founder of Virgin Group. These individuals all share a common set of characteristics, including a strong sense of purpose and direction, a willingness to take calculated risks, a growth-oriented mindset, and a commitment to continuous learning and improvement.

Another example of an individual with a wealth mindset is Sara Blakely, the founder of Spanx, a billion-dollar shapewear company. Blakely started the company with just $5,000 and a strong belief in her product. She faced numerous rejections and setbacks early on, but she persisted and eventually landed a deal with Neiman Marcus that launched her company into the spotlight. Today, Spanx is one of the most successful shapewear companies in the world, and Blakely is worth over $1 billion.

Another example is Tony Robbins, a motivational speaker, author, and entrepreneur. Robbins grew up in a challenging environment and struggled with poverty and abuse. However, he refused to let these challenges hold him back and instead focused on developing a growth-oriented mindset. Today, Robbins is one of the most sought-after motivational speakers in the world, and his books and seminars have helped millions of people achieve their goals and improve their lives.

Another successful individual with a wealth mindset is Brian Tracy, a renowned speaker and author in the field of personal and professional development. Tracy grew up in a working-class family and started his career as a door-to-door salesman. However, he was determined to achieve more and started studying the habits and behaviors of successful people. Today, Tracy is a best-selling author and has delivered seminars and training programs to millions of people around the world, helping them to achieve greater success in their personal and professional lives.

A final example of an individual with a wealth mindset is Angela Duckworth, a psychologist and author who has studied the concept of grit and its role in success. Duckworth defines grit as the combination of passion and perseverance, and she argues that it is a key factor in achieving long-term success. Duckworth's research has shown that individuals who exhibit high levels of grit are more likely to achieve their goals, even in the face of adversity and setbacks.

In conclusion, there are many examples of successful individuals who have adopted a wealth mindset and achieved great success in their lives. These individuals come from diverse backgrounds and fields, but they share a common set of characteristics, including a growth-oriented mindset, a strong sense of purpose and direction, a willingness to take risks, and a commitment to continuous learning and improvement. By studying the habits and behaviors of these successful individuals, we can learn valuable lessons about how to adopt a wealth mindset and achieve our own goals and aspirations.

Chapter 5

5.1 The Connection of Mindset and Financial Success

The connection between mindset and financial success is a topic that has been extensively researched and discussed in recent years. Many experts agree that the way we think about money and our approach to financial management can have a significant impact on our overall financial well-being.

One of the key elements of a wealth mindset is a focus on abundance rather than scarcity. People with a wealth mindset believe that there is enough money and resources to go around, and that they can create and attract abundance in their lives. This belief in abundance helps to shift their thinking away from fear and scarcity, and toward growth and opportunity.

Another important aspect of a wealth mindset is a focus on goals and the future. People with a wealth mindset are proactive in setting financial goals and creating a plan to achieve them. They understand the importance of delayed gratification and are willing to make short-term sacrifices in order to achieve long-term financial success. They also understand the power of compound interest and are willing to invest their money wisely in order to achieve their financial goals.

People with a wealth mindset are also willing to take calculated risks in order to achieve their financial goals. They understand that there is always some level of risk involved in investing and entrepreneurship, but they also understand that the potential rewards can be significant. They are willing to take on these risks in order to achieve financial freedom and independence.

One of the most important aspects of a wealth mindset is a commitment to continuous learning and improvement. People with a wealth mindset understand that financial success requires ongoing education and skill development. They are willing to invest time and money in learning about financial management, investing, and entrepreneurship in order to improve their financial knowledge and skills.

The opposite of a wealth mindset is a scarcity mindset, which is characterized by a belief that there is never enough money or resources to go around. People with a scarcity mindset often feel trapped in their current financial situation and may believe that they are not capable of achieving financial success. This mindset can lead to feelings of anxiety, stress, and hopelessness, and can make it difficult to take proactive steps toward financial improvement.

Research has shown that individuals with a wealth mindset are more likely to achieve financial success than those with a scarcity mindset. One study published in the Journal of Personality and Social Psychology found that people with a growth mindset (which is similar to a wealth mindset) were more likely to achieve financial success than those with a fixed mindset (which is similar to a scarcity mindset). The study found that the growth mindset was associated with greater financial responsibility, more effective financial management, and higher levels of financial well-being.

Another study published in the Journal of Financial Counseling and Planning found that individuals with a growth mindset were more likely to engage in financial planning and were more likely to achieve their financial goals. The study also found that individuals with a growth mindset had higher levels of financial satisfaction and were more likely to report feeling financially secure.

The mindset that one has about money and wealth can greatly impact their financial success. Those who have a positive and abundance mindset tend to attract more opportunities and resources that can help them achieve their financial goals. In contrast, individuals with a negative or scarcity mindset tend to struggle with financial difficulties and may experience limited opportunities for financial growth.

One of the main reasons why mindset plays a significant role in financial success is due to the way our minds process information and respond to external stimuli. Our thoughts, emotions, and beliefs have a direct impact on our behavior and decision-making, which can either help or hinder our financial progress.

For example, individuals with a positive mindset tend to view setbacks or failures as opportunities for growth and learning, while those with a negative mindset may give up or become discouraged when faced with obstacles. This difference in mindset can determine whether one takes action towards their financial goals or remains stagnant.

Additionally, the mindset that one has about money and wealth can influence their attitudes towards risk-taking, investment, and financial planning. Individuals with a wealth mindset tend to be more comfortable with taking calculated risks and investing in themselves and their financial future. On the other hand, those with a scarcity mindset may avoid risk-taking and may not prioritize financial planning.

Research has also shown that mindset can impact financial outcomes in various areas such as income, savings, and debt management. Individuals with a positive mindset tend to earn more income, save more money, and have better debt management skills than those with a negative mindset.

Overall, the connection between mindset and financial success is a complex and multi-dimensional relationship. However, it is clear that having a positive and abundance mindset can greatly impact one's financial success and overall well-being. By cultivating a wealth mindset and taking action towards financial goals, individuals can improve their financial outcomes and create a more fulfilling life.

In conclusion, the connection between mindset and financial success is clear. People with a wealth mindset are more likely to achieve financial success because they approach money and financial management with a positive, growth-oriented attitude. They are proactive in setting financial goals, willing to take calculated risks, committed to continuous learning and improvement, and believe that there is abundance and opportunity available to them. On the other hand, people with a scarcity mindset are more likely to struggle with financial management and may find it difficult to achieve financial success. By adopting a wealth mindset, individuals can improve their financial well-being and achieve greater financial success.

Chapter 6

6.1 How a Wealth Mindset Can Help You Achieve Your Goals?

Having a wealth mindset can greatly benefit individuals in achieving their goals, both financially and personally. A wealth mindset is characterized by a positive and abundance mindset that focuses on opportunities rather than limitations. It is a mindset that encourages growth, learning, and taking action towards achieving one's goals. In this article, we will discuss how a wealth mindset can help you achieve your goals and create a more fulfilling life.

6.2 Clear goal-setting:

A wealth mindset encourages individuals to set clear and specific goals. When individuals have a clear understanding of what they want to achieve, they are more likely to take action towards reaching their goals. A wealth mindset helps individuals to define their goals and break them down into actionable steps, which makes the process of achieving them more manageable and less overwhelming.

6.3 Growth mindset:

A wealth mindset is also characterized by a growth mindset. This means that individuals believe that they can learn, grow, and improve over time. A growth mindset encourages individuals to take risks, learn from mistakes, and use setbacks as opportunities for growth and learning. With a growth mindset, individuals can develop the skills and knowledge they need to achieve their goals and create a more fulfilling life.

6.4 Action-oriented:

A wealth mindset emphasizes taking action towards achieving one's goals. Individuals with a wealth mindset understand that their thoughts and intentions are not enough to create the life they want. They must take consistent and intentional action towards their goals. This includes taking calculated risks, making tough decisions, and being proactive in seeking out opportunities to advance towards their goals.

6.5 Self-belief:

A wealth mindset also emphasizes the importance of self-belief. Self-belief is the belief that one is capable of achieving their goals and creating the life they want. Individuals with self-belief are more likely to take risks, persevere through challenges, and stay focused on their goals. Self-belief helps individuals to overcome self-doubt and limiting beliefs that may hold them back from achieving their goals.

6.6 Focus on growth and contribution:

A wealth mindset also encourages individuals to focus on growth and contribution. This means that individuals are not only focused on achieving their own goals but also on contributing to the world in a positive way. By focusing on growth and contribution, individuals can create a sense of purpose and fulfillment that goes beyond achieving financial success.

6.7 Positive attitude:

A wealth mindset emphasizes the importance of having a positive attitude towards one's goals. This attitude helps individuals to maintain focus, motivation, and determination towards their goals, even in the face of challenges or setbacks. A positive attitude also helps individuals to attract opportunities and resources that can help them achieve their goals.

6.8 Resilience:

A wealth mindset also emphasizes resilience. Resilience is the ability to bounce back from setbacks or failures and continue moving towards one's goals. Resilience is essential in achieving goals because setbacks and failures are inevitable. Individuals with a wealth mindset understand that setbacks and failures are part of the process and use them as opportunities for growth and learning.

6.9 Develop a strong work ethic:

People with a wealth mindset understand that success requires hard work and dedication. They have a strong work ethic and are willing to put in the effort required to achieve their goals. They prioritize their time and focus on the activities that will bring them closer to their goals.

6.10 Seek out mentors and role models:

Wealth mindset individuals understand the value of learning from those who have already achieved success. They seek out mentors and role models who can provide guidance and advice on their journey to success.

6.11 Visualize success:

Visualization is a powerful tool that can help individuals achieve their goals. Wealth mindset individuals use visualization to imagine themselves achieving their goals, and the positive emotions associated with that achievement. This visualization helps to create a positive mental image of the desired outcome, making it more likely to happen.

6.12 Practice gratitude:

Gratitude is a powerful emotion that can help individuals maintain a positive attitude and focus on the good things in life. Wealth mindset individuals practice gratitude by acknowledging their accomplishments, celebrating small wins, and expressing gratitude for the people and opportunities in their lives.

6.13 Develop a sense of purpose:

People with a wealth mindset understand that true success comes from living a purposeful life. They have a clear sense of their values, passions, and purpose, and align their goals and actions accordingly. This sense of purpose provides motivation and direction, helping individuals to stay focused on their goals.

6.14 Give back to others:

Wealth mindset individuals understand the importance of giving back to others. They use their success to make a positive impact on the world by contributing to causes they care about, volunteering their time, or mentoring others.

In summary, by adopting a wealth mindset, individuals can unlock their full potential and achieve their dreams. By incorporating these principles into their lives, individuals can achieve their goals, live a purposeful life, and make a

Chapter 7

7.1 Why Mindset Matters More than Money

Money is undoubtedly an important factor when it comes to achieving financial success. However, research has shown that mindset matters more than money in determining an individual's financial success. In this article, we will explore why mindset is more important than money and how adopting a wealth mindset can help individuals achieve their financial goals.

7.2 Mindset shapes our actions and decisions:

Our mindset shapes the way we think, act and make decisions. It influences the goals we set for ourselves and the actions we take to achieve them. If we have a mindset focused solely on making money, we may make decisions that prioritize short-term gains over long-term success. However, if we have a wealth mindset, we are more likely to make decisions that align with our values, purpose, and long-term goals.

7.3 Mindset determines our relationship with money:

Our mindset also shapes our relationship with money. Individuals with a poverty mindset tend to see money as scarce and difficult to attain. They may view wealth as something reserved for a select few and may be more likely to spend money impulsively or hold onto it tightly, fearing that it may run out. On the other hand, individuals with a wealth mindset view money as a tool for creating opportunities and building a better life. They understand the value of investing, saving, and giving back to others.

Mindset impacts our ability to handle setbacks:

Setbacks and failures are an inevitable part of any journey towards success. Individuals with a poverty mindset may view setbacks as proof that they will never be successful, leading them to give up on their goals. On the other hand, individuals with a wealth mindset view setbacks as opportunities for growth and learning. They are resilient, adaptable and willing to learn from their failures, using them as stepping stones towards their goals.

7.4 Mindset determines our level of motivation and drive:

Motivation and drive are critical factors in achieving financial success. Individuals with a poverty mindset may lack motivation and drive, believing that their efforts will never pay off. They may feel discouraged by the challenges they face and lack the energy to keep going. However, individuals with a wealth mindset are highly motivated and driven, seeing challenges as opportunities for growth and pushing themselves to overcome obstacles.

7.5 Mindset shapes our perception of success:

The way we define success has a significant impact on our ability to achieve it. Individuals with a poverty mindset may view success solely in terms of material possessions or financial gains. However, individuals with a wealth mindset understand that true success comes from living a purposeful life and making a positive impact on the world. They prioritize their values, passions, and purpose, and use their success to create opportunities and give back to others.

7.6 Money is not a guarantee of success:

While having financial resources can certainly make achieving certain goals easier, it's important to remember that wealth alone is not enough to guarantee success. Without the right mindset, even those with significant financial resources can struggle to achieve their goals.

7.7 Mindset can help you make better financial decisions:

When you have a wealth mindset, you are more likely to make smart financial decisions that will help you build and maintain wealth over the long term. This might include things like investing wisely, avoiding debt, and developing a disciplined savings plan.

7.8 Mindset can help you overcome obstacles:

No matter how much money you have, there will always be obstacles and challenges that stand in the way of success. However, with the right mindset, you can develop the resilience and persistence needed to overcome these obstacles and achieve your goals.

7.9 Mindset can help you stay motivated:

Building wealth and achieving financial success can be a long and challenging journey. Without the right mindset, it's easy to get discouraged and give up when things get tough. However, when you have a wealth mindset, you are more likely to stay motivated and keep pushing forward even when the going gets tough.

7.10 Mindset can help you build meaningful relationships:

Building wealth is not just about making money, it's also about building relationships and creating a strong support network. When you have a wealth mindset, you are more likely to develop the communication, leadership, and interpersonal skills needed to build strong relationships with others.

Overall, the key takeaway is that mindset plays a critical role in determining success, both financially and in other areas of life. While money certainly has its place, it is ultimately your mindset that will determine whether or not you are able to achieve your goals and live the life you truly want. By adopting a wealth mindset and focusing on building the skills, habits, and attitudes that lead to success, you can create a life of abundance and fulfillment, regardless of your financial situation.

In conclusion, while money is undoubtedly an important factor in achieving financial success, mindset matters more. Adopting a wealth mindset can help individuals make better decisions, build a positive relationship with money, handle setbacks, maintain motivation and drive, and define success on their own terms. By focusing on mindset, individuals can achieve their financial goals while also creating a purposeful and fulfilling life.

Chapter 8

8.1 The Importance of Taking Action

Taking action is a critical component of achieving success in any area of life, including when it comes to building wealth and achieving financial goals. Without action, even the most well-crafted plans and goals are nothing more than ideas and dreams. In this section, we'll explore why taking action is so important and how you can develop the habits and mindset needed to take action and achieve your goals.

8.2 Action is the key to progress:

At its core, taking action is simply a matter of making progress towards your goals. Whether you're trying to start a business, invest in the stock market, or simply save money for a rainy day, taking action is what allows you to move forward and make progress towards your objectives.

8.3 Action is essential for learning and growth:

When you take action, you are able to learn from your experiences and grow as a person. This might mean learning from your mistakes, trying new things, or pushing yourself outside of your comfort zone in order to learn and grow.

8.4 Action breeds confidence:

When you take action and see results, it builds confidence and reinforces the belief that you are capable of achieving your goals. On the other hand, if you don't take action, you can quickly lose confidence and begin to doubt your abilities and potential.

8.5 Action creates momentum:

Once you start taking action towards your goals, it creates a positive feedback loop that can help you build momentum and keep moving forward. As you see progress and results, it becomes easier to stay motivated and continue taking action, which in turn leads to even more progress and success.

8.6 Action is necessary for success:

Ultimately, success is not achieved by simply thinking about your goals or dreaming about what you want to achieve - it is achieved through taking consistent, focused action over time. Whether you're trying to build wealth, start a business, or achieve any other type of goal, taking action is an essential component of success.

So, how can you develop the habits and mindset needed to take action and achieve your goals? Here are a few tips:

8.7 Break your goals into small, manageable steps:

One of the biggest obstacles to taking action is feeling overwhelmed by the sheer size or scope of your goals. To overcome this, try breaking your goals into smaller, more manageable steps that you can tackle one at a time.

8.8 Set deadlines and hold yourself accountable:

It's easy to procrastinate or put off taking action when there are no immediate consequences. To combat this, set deadlines for yourself and hold yourself accountable for meeting them.

8.9 Focus on progress, not perfection:

Perfectionism can be a major barrier to taking action. Instead of striving for perfection, focus on making progress towards your goals, even if it's not always perfect or exactly what you had in mind.

8.10 Visualize your success:

Visualization is a powerful tool for building motivation and confidence. Take time to visualize yourself taking action and achieving your goals, and focus on the positive feelings and outcomes that will come from that success.

8.11 Surround yourself with supportive people:

Finally, surround yourself with people who will support and encourage you as you take action towards your goals. Having a strong support network can make all the difference when it comes to staying motivated and pushing through challenges and setbacks.

There are several reasons why taking action is so important. First and foremost, action leads to results. You can have the best mindset in the world, but without taking action, you will not see any tangible benefits. By taking action, you can start to see progress toward your goals, which will motivate you to keep going.

Second, taking action helps you to learn and grow. When you take action, you will encounter obstacles and challenges along the way. This is a natural part of the learning process, and it is through overcoming these challenges that you will gain valuable experience and knowledge. With each challenge you overcome, you will become better equipped to handle future obstacles.

Third, taking action helps you to build momentum. Once you start taking action toward your goals, you will begin to build momentum. This momentum will make it easier for you to take further action and will create a sense of positive momentum that will carry you forward.

Finally, taking action helps you to develop discipline and persistence. When you commit to taking action, you are developing the discipline and persistence needed to achieve your goals. These qualities are essential for success in any endeavor, and they will serve you well in all areas of your life.

In conclusion, taking action is a critical component of achieving success, both financially and in other areas of life. By breaking your goals into manageable steps, setting deadlines and holding yourself accountable, focusing on progress, visualizing success, and surrounding yourself with supportive people, you can develop the habits and mindset needed to take action and achieve your goals.

In summary, taking action is critical to achieving success with a wealth mindset. Without action, your mindset alone will not be enough to bring you the results you desire. By taking action, you can start to see progress toward your goals, learn and grow, build momentum, and develop the discipline and persistence needed to achieve your dreams.

Chapter 9

9.1 Developing a Positive Attitude Toward Wealth and Success

Developing a positive attitude toward wealth and success is essential for achieving your financial goals. Your mindset is a powerful tool that can either help or hinder your progress, so it's important to cultivate a positive attitude if you want to succeed.

Here are some tips for developing a positive attitude toward wealth and success:

9.2 Believe in Yourself:

One of the most important things you can do to develop a positive attitude is to believe in yourself. Believe that you are capable of achieving great things and that you deserve to be successful. Avoid negative self-talk and instead focus on your strengths and abilities.

9.3 Surround Yourself with Positive People:

The people you surround yourself with can have a significant impact on your attitude. Surround yourself with positive, supportive people who believe in you and your goals. Avoid negative people who try to bring you down or discourage you.

9.4 Practice Gratitude:

Cultivating a sense of gratitude can help you develop a more positive attitude. Take time each day to focus on the things you are grateful for, no matter how small they may seem. This can help you shift your focus from what you lack to what you already have.

9.5 Visualize Success:

Visualization is a powerful tool for developing a positive attitude. Take time each day to visualize yourself achieving your financial goals. Imagine what it will feel like to have the wealth and success you desire. This can help you stay motivated and focused on your goals.

9.6 Embrace Challenges:

Instead of fearing challenges, embrace them as opportunities for growth. Challenges are a natural part of the process of achieving success, and they can help you develop the skills and knowledge you need to succeed. Embracing challenges with a positive attitude can help you overcome obstacles and achieve your goals.

9.7 Learn from Failure:

Failure is inevitable on the path to success, but it's how you respond to failure that matters. Instead of viewing failure as a setback, view it as a learning opportunity. Analyze what went wrong and use that knowledge to make improvements and move forward.

9.8 Celebrate Your Wins:

Finally, celebrate your successes, no matter how small they may seem. Celebrating your wins can help you maintain a positive attitude and stay motivated on your journey toward wealth and success.

To develop a positive attitude toward wealth and success, you can start by examining any negative beliefs or biases you may have about money, such as the belief that money is evil or that wealthy people are greedy. Once you identify these beliefs, you can work to challenge and replace them with more positive, empowering ones.

It's also important to focus on abundance rather than scarcity. Instead of feeling like there is a limited amount of wealth and success to go around, approach it with the mindset that there is plenty to be had for everyone. This can help you feel more motivated to pursue your goals and more willing to share your knowledge and resources with others.

Another key aspect of developing a positive attitude toward wealth and success is to focus on the possibilities rather than the obstacles. Instead of getting discouraged by setbacks or challenges, see them as opportunities to learn and grow. Stay optimistic and maintain a "can-do" attitude, and you'll be better equipped to handle whatever comes your way.

Overall, developing a positive attitude toward wealth and success is an important part of cultivating a wealth mindset. By letting go of negative beliefs, focusing on abundance, and staying optimistic, you can create a mindset that is conducive to achieving financial success and building wealth over the long term.

In summary, developing a positive attitude toward wealth and success is essential for achieving your financial goals. To cultivate a positive attitude, believe in yourself, surround yourself with positive people, practice gratitude, visualize success, embrace challenges, learn from failure, and celebrate your wins. By adopting a positive attitude, you can overcome obstacles, stay motivated, and achieve the wealth and success you desire.

Chapter 10

10.1 How to Cultivate a Wealth Mindset That Works for You

Cultivating a wealth mindset is all about developing the right attitudes and beliefs to help you achieve financial success. But how exactly can you go about doing this? Here are some steps you can take to cultivate a wealth mindset that works for you:

10.2 Identify your limiting beliefs:

Start by identifying any beliefs you may have about money or wealth that are holding you back. These may be beliefs like "money is the root of all evil" or "rich people are greedy." Once you identify these beliefs, work to challenge and replace them with more positive, empowering beliefs that support your goals.

10.3 Set clear goals:

To cultivate a wealth mindset, it's important to have clear goals that you are working toward. These goals should be specific, measurable, and realistic, and they should be aligned with your values and passions. When you have clear goals in mind, you'll be better able to focus your efforts and stay motivated.

10.4 Develop a positive relationship with money:

Many people have a negative relationship with money, viewing it as something that is scarce or difficult to obtain. To cultivate a wealth mindset, it's important to develop a positive relationship with money, seeing it as a tool that can help you achieve your goals and live the life you want.

10.5 Surround yourself with positive influences:

The people you surround yourself with can have a big impact on your mindset and beliefs. To cultivate a wealth mindset, surround yourself with positive, supportive people who share your goals and values. Seek out mentors, coaches, and other successful people who can inspire and guide you on your journey.

10.6 Learn from failure:

Failure is a natural part of any journey toward success. To cultivate a wealth mindset, it's important to learn from your failures and setbacks, rather than letting them discourage you. Use your failures as opportunities to learn and grow, and use what you've learned to improve your approach and strategy moving forward.

10.7 Practice gratitude:

Cultivating a wealth mindset is not just about accumulating wealth and success - it's also about feeling grateful for what you already have. Practice gratitude on a regular basis by taking time to appreciate the good things in your life, such as your health, your relationships, and the opportunities you have to pursue your goals.

10.8 Stay focused and disciplined:

Finally, to cultivate a wealth mindset, it's important to stay focused and disciplined in your efforts. Stay true to your values and goals, and make sure that your actions are aligned with your vision for the future. Be willing to make sacrifices and put in the hard work necessary to achieve your goals, and stay committed to your journey even when things get tough.

10.9 Identify Your Money Story:

Your money story is the set of beliefs, values, and experiences you have around money that shape your attitude towards it. By identifying your money story, you can understand how it has influenced your financial decisions and start to reframe it to align with your goals.

10.10 Develop a Growth Mindset:

A growth mindset is the belief that your abilities can be developed through dedication and hard work. This is important when it comes to wealth creation because it allows you to see challenges as opportunities to learn and grow, rather than as obstacles that hold you back.

10.11 Practice Gratitude:

Gratitude is the practice of focusing on what you have, rather than what you lack. By focusing on the abundance in your life, you can shift your mindset from one of scarcity to one of abundance, which can help you attract more wealth and success.

10.12 Visualize Your Future:

Visualization is a powerful tool that can help you create the life you want. By visualizing yourself as already having achieved your financial goals, you can create a sense of certainty and conviction that will help you take the necessary actions to make your vision a reality.

10.13 Surround Yourself with Positive Influences:

The people you surround yourself with can have a significant impact on your mindset and your ability to achieve your goals. Surround yourself with positive, supportive, and like-minded people who will encourage you to pursue your dreams and challenge you to be your best self.

10.14 Take Inspired Action:

Inspired action is action that is taken from a place of alignment with your goals and values. When you take inspired action, you are motivated by passion and purpose, rather than by fear or desperation. This can help you stay focused and committed to your goals, even when the going gets tough.

By following these steps, you can cultivate a wealth mindset that works for you, helping you achieve your financial goals and live the life you want. Remember that developing a wealth mindset is a lifelong journey, and that it requires ongoing effort, focus, and discipline. But with persistence and dedication, you can create a mindset that is conducive to achieving financial success and building wealth over the long term.

Part 1 Complete

Part 2

The Importance of Goals

Goals are essential to success, and in this chapter, readers will learn how to set effective goals that align with their values and aspirations. It will provide strategies for breaking down big goals into smaller, achievable steps and for tracking progress along the way.

Chapter 1

1.1 Why Goals are Essential for Achieving Financial Success

When it comes to achieving financial success, setting and working towards goals is essential. Without goals, it can be difficult to know what you're working towards or what you need to do to get there. Here are some reasons why setting goals is important for financial success:

1.2 Provides clarity and focus:

Setting goals helps you get clear about what you want to achieve, so you can focus your time, energy, and resources towards that specific goal. This clarity can help you make better decisions about how you spend your money and time.

1.3 Keeps you motivated:

Having a specific financial goal can help keep you motivated to work towards it. When you have something to look forward to and work towards, it can help you stay focused and dedicated even when faced with challenges.

1.4 Helps measure progress:

Setting goals also helps you measure your progress along the way. You can track your progress, see how far you've come, and make adjustments to your plan if necessary.

1.5 Increases confidence:

Achieving financial goals can increase your confidence and self-esteem. This can have a positive impact on other areas of your life, such as your career, relationships, and overall well-being.

1.6 Helps you prioritize:

When you have financial goals, it can help you prioritize what's important. You may need to cut back on certain expenses or make sacrifices to achieve your goals, but having a clear understanding of what you want to achieve can help you make these decisions.

To cultivate a wealth mindset that works for you, it's important to set clear and specific financial goals. Your goals should be SMART - specific, measurable, achievable, relevant, and time-bound. This means that they should be clear and specific, so you know exactly what you're working towards. They should also be measurable, so you can track your progress along the way. It's important that your goals are achievable, so you don't become discouraged or overwhelmed. Your goals should also be relevant to your overall financial plan and aligned with your values. Finally, your goals should be time-bound, so you have a deadline to work towards.

Once you've set your financial goals, it's important to create a plan to achieve them. This plan should include specific actions you'll take to achieve your goals, as well as a timeline and milestones to track your progress. It's important to review your plan regularly, making adjustments as necessary.

In addition to setting goals and creating a plan, cultivating a wealth mindset also involves adopting a positive attitude towards money and success. This may include reframing negative beliefs about money and success, surrounding yourself with positive and supportive people, and seeking out resources and education to help you achieve your goals.

Having clear goals is essential for achieving financial success because they provide direction, focus, and motivation. Without goals, it's easy to become overwhelmed, lost, or demotivated. Setting goals helps individuals to create a roadmap for their financial journey, which includes a clear understanding of where they are, where they want to go, and how they plan to get there.

When setting financial goals, it's important to make them specific, measurable, achievable, relevant, and time-bound (SMART). For example, instead of setting a vague goal like "I want to save more money," a SMART goal would be "I want to save $10,000 in the next 12 months by reducing my expenses by 20% and increasing my income by taking on freelance work."

Having SMART goals allows individuals to break down their larger financial aspirations into manageable tasks and track their progress. By doing so, they can stay motivated, adjust their plans as necessary, and celebrate their achievements along the way.

Additionally, having goals can also help individuals prioritize their spending and make smarter financial decisions. When faced with a choice between spending money on something that aligns with their financial goals and something that doesn't, they will be more likely to choose the former. This type of discipline can lead to long-term financial success.

Finally, goals help individuals to create a sense of purpose and meaning in their financial journey. Rather than simply accumulating wealth for its own sake, having a clear purpose for that wealth can make the journey more fulfilling and rewarding. This can help individuals stay committed to their financial goals even during challenging times.

Overall, goals are an essential component of a wealth mindset. They provide direction, focus, and motivation, and help individuals prioritize their spending and make smarter financial decisions. By setting and working towards specific, measurable, achievable, relevant, and time-bound goals, individuals can achieve financial success and create a more fulfilling and purposeful life.

Chapter 2

2.1 The Characteristics of Effective Goals

The success of achieving financial goals relies heavily on setting effective goals. Effective goals are specific, measurable, attainable, relevant, and time-bound (SMART). Let's break down each of these characteristics in detail:

2.2 Specific:

An effective goal is specific and clearly defined. The more specific a goal is, the more it can be broken down into achievable steps. For example, rather than setting a vague goal like "I want to make more money," a specific goal would be "I want to increase my monthly income by 20% by the end of the year."

2.3 Measurable:

An effective goal is measurable, meaning you can track your progress and determine if you are making progress towards achieving it. For example, if your goal is to save $10,000 in a year, you can track your progress each month to ensure you are on track to meet your target.

2.4 Attainable:

An effective goal is attainable, meaning it is realistic and achievable given your current resources, skills, and time. Setting an unattainable goal can lead to frustration and discouragement. For example, setting a goal to become a billionaire within a year may not be realistic or attainable.

2.5 Relevant:

An effective goal is relevant to your overall vision and values. It should align with your personal and professional goals, and be something that motivates and inspires you. For example, if your ultimate goal is to become financially independent, setting a goal to invest in a rental property aligns with your long-term vision.

2.6 Time-bound:

An effective goal is time-bound, meaning it has a specific deadline for achievement. Setting a deadline creates urgency and helps to prioritize tasks and allocate resources. For example, if your goal is to pay off your credit card debt, setting a deadline of six months can help you stay focused and motivated.

2.7 Realistic:

Effective goals are achievable, realistic, and relevant to your overall financial plan. Setting overly ambitious goals that are unrealistic can demotivate you and undermine your overall progress.

2.8 Challenging yet attainable:

Effective goals should be challenging enough to push you beyond your comfort zone, yet still attainable with effort and persistence.

2.9 Aligned with values and purpose:

Effective goals should be aligned with your values, beliefs, and overall purpose in life. This ensures that you are pursuing financial success in a way that feels authentic and meaningful to you.

In summary, setting effective goals is an essential part of achieving financial success. A specific, measurable, attainable, relevant, and time-bound goal provides a roadmap for success and helps to stay motivated and on track.

Chapter 3

3.1 The Power of Specificity in Goal-Setting

Goal-setting is an essential part of achieving financial success and cultivating a wealth mindset. However, simply setting goals is not enough to guarantee success. The key to effective goal-setting lies in the power of specificity.

Specific goals provide a clear target to aim for and allow you to measure progress towards your desired outcome. When setting goals, it is important to be as specific as possible about what you want to achieve. Instead of setting a general goal such as "make more money," try to set a specific goal such as "increase my income by 10% by the end of the year."

The power of specificity in goal-setting is an important concept to understand when it comes to achieving financial success. Many people set vague or general goals, such as "I want to make more money," but these goals lack the detail and direction needed to make them effective. Specificity means setting goals that are clear, concise, and measurable.

When you set specific goals, you are giving yourself a roadmap for success. You know exactly what you want to achieve, how you plan to achieve it, and how you will measure your progress along the way. This clarity helps you stay focused and motivated, which in turn makes it easier to achieve your goals.

Specificity also helps you break down big goals into smaller, more manageable steps. For example, if your goal is to earn $100,000 in a year, you can break that down into monthly, weekly, and even daily goals. This makes it easier to track your progress and make adjustments as needed.

Another benefit of setting specific goals is that it helps you identify potential obstacles and come up with strategies to overcome them. When you have a clear idea of what you want to achieve and how you plan to achieve it, you can anticipate challenges that may arise and proactively address them.

When setting specific goals, it's important to consider both the short-term and long-term objectives that you want to achieve. This can help you to create a roadmap for success that outlines the steps you need to take to get where you want to go.

Specific goals also help to increase motivation and focus. When you have a clear idea of what you want to achieve, you are more likely to stay motivated and take action toward that goal. You can also use specific goals to track your progress and celebrate your successes along the way, which can help to keep you motivated over the long haul.

Specific goals can also help you to overcome obstacles and challenges. When you encounter setbacks or challenges, having a clear idea of what you're working toward can help you to stay focused and committed to your goals. You can also use your specific goals to identify the specific obstacles that are holding you back and come up with strategies to overcome them.

Another benefit of setting specific goals is that it helps to increase accountability. When you have a specific goal in mind, it's easier to hold yourself accountable for your progress and take responsibility for your own success. This can help you to stay focused and committed even when faced with distractions or competing priorities.

Finally, setting specific goals can also help you to become more resilient and adaptable. When you encounter setbacks or unexpected challenges, having a clear idea of what you want to achieve can help you to stay focused and motivated. You can also use your specific goals to adjust your plans and strategies as needed, which can help you to stay on track and continue making progress toward your long-term objectives.

Overall, the power of specificity in goal-setting cannot be overstated. By setting specific goals, you are giving yourself a clear direction for achieving financial success, breaking down big goals into manageable steps, and staying focused and motivated along the way.

Chapter 4

4.1 The Role of Planning in Goal Achievement

Goal achievement requires more than just setting goals; it requires careful planning and execution of those plans. Planning is a crucial part of achieving your goals because it allows you to break your goal down into actionable steps and make a roadmap for how you will get from where you are now to where you want to be.

The first step in planning for goal achievement is to establish a clear picture of what you want to achieve. This requires defining your goal in specific, measurable terms so that you can track your progress and hold yourself accountable. Once you have a clear understanding of what you want to achieve, you can begin to identify the steps that will get you there.

The next step is to prioritize those steps and determine which are the most critical to achieving your goal. This may involve breaking down your goal into smaller, more manageable milestones or identifying the resources you need to acquire along the way. Once you have identified the key steps, you can begin to develop a timeline and schedule for completing them.

Planning also involves assessing any potential obstacles or challenges that may arise and developing strategies for overcoming them. This may involve anticipating potential setbacks and developing contingency plans, or seeking out additional resources or support that will help you stay on track.

It's important to remember that planning is not a one-time activity; it is an ongoing process that requires constant evaluation and adjustment. As you work towards your goals, you may find that your plans need to be revised or refined based on new information or changing circumstances. By remaining flexible and adaptable, you can ensure that your plans remain relevant and effective.

Planning involves breaking down your goals into smaller, more manageable steps, and then figuring out what you need to do to achieve each step. Planning helps you stay organized and focused, and it gives you a roadmap to follow as you work towards your goals.

One of the most important aspects of planning is creating a timeline. You need to set specific deadlines for each step along the way to ensure that you're making progress and staying on track. Without deadlines, it's easy to get sidetracked or lose motivation.

Another key aspect of planning is identifying potential obstacles and coming up with solutions to overcome them. This helps you anticipate potential challenges and plan accordingly, so you're better equipped to deal with them when they arise.

Effective planning also involves monitoring your progress and adjusting your plan as needed. This means regularly reviewing your goals and the steps you're taking to achieve them, and making adjustments based on your progress and any changes in your circumstances.

In addition to these practical aspects of planning, it's important to approach planning with the right mindset. This means staying open to new ideas and being willing to adapt your plan as needed, while also remaining focused and disciplined in pursuing your goals.

Ultimately, planning is an important component of goal achievement, and it requires both practical skills and a positive mindset. By taking the time to plan out your goals and breaking them down into manageable steps, you can stay focused, motivated, and on track as you work towards achieving financial success.

In conclusion, planning is a crucial part of achieving your goals, and a key element in cultivating a wealth mindset. By taking the time to establish clear, specific goals, prioritize your actions, and develop a plan for achieving them, you can increase your chances of success and build the foundation for a lifetime of financial prosperity.

Chapter 5

5.1 Strategies for Staying Accountable to Your Goals

Staying accountable to your goals is crucial for achieving success. Without accountability, it is easy to get sidetracked and lose focus. However, with the right strategies, it is possible to stay on track and achieve your goals.

One effective strategy is to share your goals with someone who can hold you accountable. This could be a friend, family member, or even a coach. By sharing your goals with someone, you are making a commitment to yourself and to them, which can be a powerful motivator.

Another strategy is to set regular check-ins for yourself. This could be a weekly or monthly review of your progress towards your goals. During these check-ins, you can assess what has been working well and what needs improvement. You can also adjust your plan as needed to ensure that you are on track to achieving your goals.

Using a journal or planner to track your progress can also be helpful. Write down your goals and break them down into smaller, achievable tasks. Then, check off each task as you complete it. This will give you a sense of accomplishment and help you stay motivated.

It is also important to celebrate your successes along the way. When you achieve a milestone or make significant progress towards your goal, take time to acknowledge and celebrate your achievement. This will help you stay motivated and focused on your end goal.

Another useful strategy is to set up a system of rewards and consequences. For example, you might reward yourself with a special treat or activity when you achieve a milestone or goal, or you might set consequences for failing to meet a deadline or goal.

It's also important to regularly review your progress and adjust your strategies as needed. This can involve tracking your progress towards your goals, identifying areas where you may be struggling, and brainstorming new approaches or solutions to help you overcome obstacles.

Finally, it can be helpful to surround yourself with a supportive community of people who share your goals and values. This might involve joining a group or organization related to your area of focus, attending workshops or conferences, or seeking out mentors or coaches who can provide guidance and support. By staying connected to a community of like-minded individuals, you can stay inspired and motivated on your journey towards achieving your goals.

Chapter 6

6.1 Adjusting Goals as You Progress Toward Financial Success

Adjusting goals as you progress toward financial success is an important part of achieving your financial objectives. Goals should not be set in stone and must be flexible enough to allow for changes based on new information, changing circumstances, and other factors. This chapter will discuss the importance of adjusting goals and provide strategies for doing so effectively.

One of the primary reasons why it is important to adjust goals as you progress toward financial success is that circumstances often change. Economic conditions, family situations, and other factors can all affect your ability to achieve your original goals. When circumstances change, it is important to reassess your goals and adjust them as needed. This can help ensure that you stay on track and continue to make progress toward your financial objectives.

Another reason why it is important to adjust goals is that they can become outdated or irrelevant. As you learn more about the financial markets and gain a better understanding of your own financial situation, you may discover that your original goals were not realistic or achievable. In these cases, it is important to adjust your goals to reflect your new understanding and to set more realistic targets.

One strategy for adjusting goals is to regularly review your progress and reassess your objectives. This can be done on a monthly or quarterly basis, depending on the complexity of your financial situation and the nature of your goals. During these reviews, you should evaluate your progress, assess the current economic conditions and other factors affecting your financial situation, and adjust your goals as needed.

Another strategy for adjusting goals is to seek feedback and advice from trusted advisors, such as financial planners or investment professionals. These experts can help you evaluate your progress and make recommendations for adjustments to your goals or investment strategy. Additionally, they can provide valuable insight into the financial markets and help you navigate complex financial situations.

When adjusting goals, it is important to be flexible and open to change. This means being willing to let go of old goals and setting new targets that are more realistic and achievable. It also means being willing to make changes to your investment strategy or financial plan if necessary.

In order to effectively adjust goals, it is important to have a clear understanding of your financial situation and your long-term objectives. This requires a comprehensive financial plan that takes into account your current income, expenses, assets, and liabilities, as well as your long-term financial goals. A financial plan can help you stay focused on your objectives and provide a roadmap for achieving them.

In conclusion, adjusting goals as you progress toward financial success is an important part of achieving your financial objectives. Goals should be flexible enough to allow for changes based on new information and changing circumstances. Strategies for adjusting goals include regularly reviewing progress and seeking advice from trusted advisors. To effectively adjust goals, it is important to have a clear understanding of your financial situation and your long-term objectives.

Chapter 7

7.1 The Connection Between Your Values and Financial Goals

The connection between your values and financial goals is an important aspect of achieving financial success. Values are beliefs and principles that are important to you and guide your behavior and decision-making. Your financial goals should be aligned with your values to ensure that you are pursuing goals that are meaningful to you and consistent with your principles.

One way to identify your values is to reflect on what is most important to you in life. This could be your relationships, your health, your personal growth, your spirituality, or other areas. Consider what you want your life to look like and what kind of person you want to be. Your values will likely reflect these aspirations.

Once you have identified your values, you can use them to guide your financial goals. For example, if your value is to prioritize your health, you might set financial goals related to paying for gym memberships, healthy food options, or preventative healthcare measures. If your value is to prioritize personal growth, you might set financial goals related to investing in education or attending seminars and conferences.

When your financial goals are aligned with your values, you are more likely to be motivated to achieve them. You will have a deeper sense of purpose and meaning in pursuing your goals, which can help you stay committed and focused. You may also find that achieving your financial goals in alignment with your values leads to a greater sense of fulfillment and satisfaction.

To begin, start by reflecting on what matters most to you in life. What are your core values? For example, do you value security, freedom, or creativity? Once you have identified your values, you can then examine how they relate to your financial goals. For instance, if your core value is security, you may prioritize saving for a rainy day or investing in stable, long-term investments. If your core value is creativity, you may prioritize investing in your business or pursuing a career that allows you to express your creative side.

Aligning your financial goals with your values can also help you stay motivated and focused on achieving those goals. When your financial goals are aligned with your values, you are more likely to stay committed and persevere through challenges and setbacks. This is because your goals are no longer just about accumulating wealth or achieving financial success, but about fulfilling your deepest values and desires.

In addition, aligning your financial goals with your values can help you make better decisions about money. For example, if you value sustainability, you may prioritize investing in environmentally-friendly companies or choosing products that are eco-friendly. If you value social responsibility, you may prioritize donating a portion of your income to charity or investing in companies that align with your values.

Moreover, aligning your financial goals with your values can help you live a more fulfilling life. When your financial goals are aligned with your values, you are not only pursuing financial success, but also a life that is meaningful and fulfilling. This can lead to a sense of purpose and satisfaction in life that is not solely tied to financial wealth.

On the other hand, if your financial goals are not aligned with your values, you may find it challenging to stay motivated and committed. You may feel like you are pursuing goals that are not meaningful to you, which can lead to frustration and burnout.

To sum up, the connection between your values and financial goals is crucial for achieving financial success. By aligning your financial goals with your values, you can stay motivated, make better decisions, and live a more fulfilling life. It is important to take the time to reflect on your values and ensure that your financial goals are aligned with what truly matters to you.

In summary, the connection between your values and financial goals is an important consideration in achieving financial success. By identifying your values and using them to guide your financial goals, you can create a deeper sense of purpose and meaning in your financial pursuits. This can help you stay motivated and committed as you work towards achieving your financial goals.

Part 2 Complete

Part 3

Overcoming Limiting Beliefs

Many people have limiting beliefs that hold them back from achieving their full potential. In this part, you will learn how to identify and overcome these beliefs, replacing them with positive, empowering beliefs that support their financial success.

Chapter 1

1.1 Understanding Limiting Beliefs and How They Impact Your Finances

Limiting beliefs are deeply ingrained assumptions or beliefs about oneself, others, or the world that can hold people back from achieving their goals. These beliefs are often formed during childhood and can be reinforced by life experiences, societal conditioning, or negative self-talk.

When it comes to finances, limiting beliefs can have a significant impact on a person's ability to achieve financial success. For example, someone who has grown up with the belief that "money is the root of all evil" may struggle to accumulate wealth because they subconsciously view money as something negative. Or, someone who has a belief that "rich people are greedy and selfish" may sabotage their own efforts to achieve financial success because they don't want to be perceived as greedy or selfish.

Limiting beliefs can also manifest in other ways that impact financial success. For example, someone who believes that they are not good with numbers may avoid budgeting or financial planning, leading to a lack of financial organization and missed opportunities for growth. Similarly, someone who believes that they are not worthy of financial success may shy away from negotiating for higher pay or seeking out opportunities for career advancement.

To overcome limiting beliefs and achieve financial success, it's important to identify and challenge these beliefs. This can be done through self-reflection, therapy, or working with a financial coach or mentor. By recognizing and addressing limiting beliefs, individuals can begin to shift their mindset and open themselves up to new opportunities for growth and success.

In addition to challenging limiting beliefs, it's important to develop positive affirmations and visualizations that support financial success. These can help to reprogram the subconscious mind and reinforce positive beliefs about oneself and one's ability to achieve financial goals. For example, regularly affirming "I am capable of achieving financial success" or visualizing oneself living the life of their dreams can help to create a mindset that is conducive to financial growth and success.

Understanding limiting beliefs and how they impact your finances is crucial for developing a wealth mindset.

Limiting beliefs are negative thought patterns that hold you back from achieving your goals and living the life you want. When it comes to finances, limiting beliefs can have a significant impact on your ability to create wealth and achieve financial success.

Limiting beliefs often stem from past experiences, cultural or societal conditioning, or self-doubt. For example, if you grew up hearing phrases like "money doesn't grow on trees" or "rich people are greedy," you may have developed a limiting belief that money is scarce or that wealth is inherently negative. These beliefs can lead to self-sabotage or a fear of success that can hold you back from pursuing opportunities that could lead to financial growth.

To overcome limiting beliefs, it is important to identify them first. Start by examining your thoughts and feelings about money and wealth. Ask yourself what you believe about money and whether those beliefs are helping or hindering your financial goals. Once you have identified your limiting beliefs, challenge them by looking for evidence to the contrary. For example, if you believe that all wealthy people are greedy, look for examples of wealthy individuals who use their wealth for good causes or who give generously to charity.

Another way to overcome limiting beliefs is through positive affirmations. These are positive statements that you repeat to yourself regularly to reinforce positive beliefs and dispel negative ones. For example, you might say to yourself, "I am capable of creating wealth" or "Money flows easily and abundantly to me."

It is also important to surround yourself with positive influences. Seek out mentors or role models who have achieved financial success and who can provide guidance and support as you work towards your own goals. Joining a community of like-minded individuals can also be helpful for staying motivated and accountable.

Finally, it is important to take action towards your financial goals despite any limiting beliefs you may have. As you take action and experience success, your limiting beliefs will begin to fade, and you will develop a stronger wealth mindset. Remember that you are in control of your thoughts and beliefs, and by shifting your mindset towards abundance and positivity, you can overcome any limiting beliefs and achieve financial success.

Ultimately, understanding and addressing limiting beliefs is a crucial step in achieving financial success. By identifying and challenging these beliefs, individuals can begin to shift their mindset and open themselves up to new opportunities for growth and success.

Chapter 2

2.1 Common Limiting Beliefs About Money and Wealth

Common limiting beliefs about money and wealth are the negative thoughts and attitudes that people have about finances that prevent them from achieving their financial goals. Here are some of the most common limiting beliefs:

2.2 Money is the root of all evil:

This belief suggests that money is a bad thing and can lead to negative outcomes. People who hold this belief may have a negative attitude toward money and may feel guilty or ashamed about having wealth.

2.3 Money doesn't grow on trees:

This belief suggests that money is scarce and difficult to come by. People who hold this belief may feel that there is never enough money to go around and that they have to work extremely hard to earn it.

2.4 I'll never be rich:

This belief suggests that wealth is unattainable and out of reach. People who hold this belief may not set ambitious financial goals or may sabotage their efforts to build wealth.

2.5 It's selfish to want money:

This belief suggests that wanting money is a selfish and greedy desire. People who hold this belief may feel guilty about wanting to build wealth or may feel that it is not in alignment with their values.

2.6 Rich people are unhappy:

This belief suggests that wealth does not bring happiness or fulfillment. People who hold this belief may not prioritize financial success or may not believe that they can be happy if they are wealthy.

2.7 Wealth is only for the lucky or privileged:

Some people believe that wealth is only attainable for those who are born into it or who have been fortunate enough to come across opportunities that others have not. This limiting belief can prevent people from taking risks or pursuing their financial goals, as they do not see themselves as being capable of achieving success.

2.8 Money can't buy happiness:

While it is true that money cannot buy happiness, many people use this as a justification for not pursuing financial success. This limiting belief can prevent people from setting financial goals and working towards achieving them.

2.9 I'm not good with money:

Some people believe that they are simply not good with money and cannot manage it effectively. This limiting belief can prevent people from taking control of their finances and making positive changes to their financial situation.

2.10 There's never enough money:

Some people believe that no matter how much money they have, it will never be enough. This limiting belief can prevent people from feeling satisfied with their financial situation, as they constantly strive for more money without appreciating what they already have.

These limiting beliefs can prevent people from taking action and making progress toward their financial goals. It's important to identify and challenge these beliefs in order to develop a positive mindset and achieve financial success.

It is important to recognize and address these limiting beliefs in order to overcome them and achieve financial success. By shifting your mindset and adopting a more positive and empowering belief system, you can overcome these obstacles and reach your financial goals.

Chapter 3

3.1 How to Identify Your Own Limiting Beliefs

Identifying your own limiting beliefs is a crucial step in overcoming them and creating a wealth mindset. Here are some tips to help you identify your own limiting beliefs:

3.2 Pay attention to your thoughts:

To identify your limiting beliefs is to become aware of your thoughts and emotions. Pay attention to the thoughts that come to mind when you think about money and wealth. Do you feel anxious, stressed, or inadequate? Do you believe that money is the root of all evil, or that wealthy people are selfish and greedy? These are common limiting beliefs that can hold you back from achieving financial success.

Once you have identified your limiting beliefs, it's important to challenge them. Ask yourself if your beliefs are based on facts or on assumptions. Are they based on your personal experiences or on the experiences of others? Try to reframe your beliefs in a more positive and empowering way.

For example, if you believe that money is the root of all evil, challenge this belief by reminding yourself that money is simply a tool that can be used for good or bad. If you believe that wealthy people are selfish and greedy, challenge this belief by acknowledging that there are many wealthy people who are generous and use their wealth to help others.

3.3 Analyze your past experiences:

Look at your past experiences and how they have shaped your beliefs about money and wealth. Have you experienced financial difficulties in the past that have led you to believe that you are not capable of achieving financial success? Have you been raised with negative attitudes toward money and wealth? Understanding how your past experiences have influenced your beliefs can help you to challenge and overcome them.

3.4 Consider your current beliefs:

Take a moment to think about your current beliefs around money and wealth. Do you believe that you can create financial abundance in your life? Do you believe that you deserve to be wealthy? If you have any doubts or negative beliefs, it's important to address them in order to create a positive and empowering mindset.

3.5 Seek feedback from others:

Sometimes, it can be difficult to see our own limiting beliefs. Ask a trusted friend or mentor for feedback on your beliefs and thought patterns. They may be able to offer a new perspective and help you identify any limiting beliefs that you may not have recognized on your own.

It can also be helpful in identifying your limiting beliefs. Ask trusted friends, family members, or a therapist to provide you with honest feedback on your attitudes toward money and wealth. They may be able to identify patterns or beliefs that you may not be aware of.

Finally, taking action toward your financial goals can also help you to identify and overcome limiting beliefs. When you take action and see progress, you may realize that your beliefs were holding you back from achieving success. This can help you to develop a more positive and empowering mindset that supports your financial success.

In conclusion, identifying your limiting beliefs about money and wealth is an important step in achieving financial success. By becoming aware of your thoughts and emotions, challenging your beliefs, understanding how your past experiences have influenced your attitudes, seeking feedback from others, and taking action toward your goals, you can overcome limiting beliefs and develop a mindset that supports your financial success.

Chapter 4

4.1 The Power of Reframing Negative Thoughts and Beliefs

Negative thoughts and beliefs can be incredibly damaging to our financial success. They can hold us back from taking risks, pursuing opportunities, and achieving our goals. That's why it's essential to reframe negative thoughts and beliefs into positive ones that empower us rather than hold us back.

Reframing is the process of taking a negative thought or belief and transforming it into a positive one. It's about changing the way we think and the language we use to describe ourselves, our situations, and our possibilities. By reframing negative thoughts and beliefs, we can shift our mindset and cultivate a more positive outlook on our finances.

For example, let's say you have a negative belief that you're not good with money. You might reframe that belief by saying, "I am capable of managing my finances well, and I'm learning more every day." By reframing your negative belief into a positive one, you're empowering yourself to take action and improve your financial situation.

Reframing negative thoughts and beliefs can also help us overcome obstacles and setbacks. Instead of getting stuck in a negative mindset, we can reframe the situation as a learning opportunity and a chance to grow. By viewing challenges as opportunities, we're more likely to stay motivated and focused on our goals.

One way to reframe negative thoughts is to challenge them with evidence. For example, if you believe that you will never be able to save enough money to retire comfortably, you could challenge that belief by looking for evidence to the contrary. You may realize that you have already taken steps towards saving for retirement, or that you have a strong work ethic that will enable you to earn more money in the future.

Another way to reframe negative thoughts is to focus on the positive aspects of a situation. For example, if you are struggling to pay off debt, instead of feeling overwhelmed by the amount of debt you have, you could focus on the progress you have already made. By reframing your thoughts to focus on your accomplishments, you can build momentum towards achieving your financial goals.

In addition to reframing negative thoughts and beliefs, it is also important to practice gratitude. Gratitude can help shift your focus away from what you lack and towards what you have. When you focus on what you are grateful for, you will begin to notice more opportunities to grow and improve your financial situation.

Finally, it is important to practice self-compassion when you are working to reframe negative thoughts and beliefs. Changing your mindset is a process, and it is natural to encounter setbacks and challenges along the way. By treating yourself with kindness and compassion, you can maintain a positive outlook and stay motivated towards achieving your financial goals.

Ultimately, the power of reframing negative thoughts and beliefs lies in our ability to control our own mindset. By choosing to focus on the positive aspects of our financial situation, we can cultivate a wealth mindset that empowers us to achieve our goals and live the life we want.

Chapter 5

5.1 How to Challenge Limiting Beliefs and Replace Them with Empowering Beliefs

Limiting beliefs can be deeply ingrained in our subconscious minds and may have been formed as a result of our upbringing, experiences, or societal conditioning. However, it is possible to challenge and replace these limiting beliefs with more empowering ones that support our financial goals and success.

The first step in challenging limiting beliefs is to become aware of them. This requires some introspection and reflection on our thoughts and beliefs about money and wealth. It can be helpful to write down any negative thoughts or beliefs that come to mind and identify the root cause or origin of these beliefs.

Once we have identified our limiting beliefs, we can begin to challenge them by asking ourselves whether they are actually true or if there is evidence to support them. We can also examine the impact that these beliefs have on our lives and finances and consider whether they are helping or hindering us in achieving our goals.

To replace limiting beliefs with empowering ones, we can use techniques such as positive affirmations, visualization, and cognitive restructuring. Positive affirmations involve repeating positive statements to ourselves that reinforce our desired beliefs and goals. Visualization involves imagining ourselves achieving our goals and experiencing the positive emotions associated with this achievement. Cognitive restructuring involves actively challenging negative thoughts and beliefs and replacing them with more positive and empowering ones.

For example, if we have a limiting belief that "money is the root of all evil," we can challenge this belief by examining whether it is actually true and whether it is helping or hindering us in achieving our financial goals. We can then replace this belief with an empowering one such as "money is a tool that can be used for good and can help me achieve my goals."

It is important to note that replacing limiting beliefs with empowering ones is a process that takes time and practice. It requires a willingness to challenge our own beliefs and an openness to new ideas and perspectives. However, the benefits of doing so can be significant, as we can unlock our full potential and achieve greater financial success and abundance.

Challenging limiting beliefs and replacing them with empowering beliefs can be a powerful tool in cultivating a wealth mindset. The following steps can help in this process:

5.2 Identify the limiting belief:

The first step in challenging a limiting belief is to identify it. This involves becoming aware of the negative self-talk and the beliefs that hold you back. It is important to question the validity of these beliefs and understand where they come from.

5.3 Challenge the belief:

Once you have identified the limiting belief, the next step is to challenge it. This involves questioning the validity of the belief and looking for evidence to support or refute it. For example, if your limiting belief is that "money is the root of all evil", you could challenge this belief by looking for evidence of people who have used their wealth to make a positive impact in the world.

5.4 Replace the belief:

After challenging the limiting belief, the next step is to replace it with an empowering belief. This involves creating a positive and affirming statement that supports your financial goals. For example, if your limiting belief is "I will never be rich", you could replace it with an empowering belief such as "I am capable of creating abundance and wealth in my life."

5.5 Practice the new belief:

Once you have identified and replaced the limiting belief, the final step is to practice the new empowering belief. This involves repeating the new belief to yourself on a regular basis, especially when negative self-talk and limiting beliefs arise. Over time, the new empowering belief will become a part of your subconscious and help to reinforce your wealth mindset.

In addition to these steps, it can also be helpful to surround yourself with people who support your new empowering beliefs and to seek out positive affirmations and visualization exercises to reinforce your mindset.

By challenging and replacing limiting beliefs with empowering ones, you can begin to shift your mindset towards abundance and financial success. This can help you to set and achieve your financial goals and create the life of your dreams.

Chapter 6

6.1 Techniques for Overcoming Fear and Doubt About Your Financial Future

Fear and doubt are common emotions that can hold individuals back from achieving their financial goals. They can stem from limiting beliefs, past experiences, or uncertainty about the future. However, there are various techniques that can help individuals overcome these feelings and move towards financial success.

6.2 Practice Mindfulness:

Mindfulness involves being present and aware of the current moment. By focusing on the present, individuals can reduce anxiety and worry about the future. Techniques such as meditation, deep breathing, and visualization can help individuals develop mindfulness and reduce feelings of fear and doubt.

6.3 Educate Yourself:

A lack of knowledge or understanding about finances can contribute to fear and doubt. By educating yourself about personal finance and investing, you can increase your confidence and reduce your fears. Attend workshops, read books, or take online courses to learn about financial topics that interest you.

6.4 Seek Support:

Talking to a trusted friend, family member, or financial advisor can help you gain perspective and overcome fears. They can offer encouragement and guidance to help you move towards your financial goals.

6.5 Set Realistic Goals:

Setting realistic and achievable financial goals can help reduce feelings of doubt and uncertainty. Break your goals down into smaller, more manageable steps and celebrate each milestone as you progress.

6.6 Take Action:

Taking action towards your financial goals can help you build confidence and reduce fear. Start with small steps, such as creating a budget or opening a savings account, and gradually work towards more significant financial milestones.

6.7 Challenge Negative Self-Talk:

Negative self-talk can reinforce feelings of fear and doubt. Challenge negative thoughts by asking yourself if they are based on fact or assumption. Replace negative self-talk with positive affirmations and focus on your strengths and accomplishments.

6.8 Visualize Success:

Visualizing yourself achieving your financial goals can help you overcome fear and doubt. Imagine yourself living the life you want and achieving your financial dreams. Visualize the steps you need to take to get there and focus on the positive feelings associated with achieving your goals.

6.9 Take Risks:

Taking calculated risks can help you overcome fear and build confidence. Start small and gradually take bigger risks as you become more comfortable. Remember that failure is a natural part of the learning process, and it can provide valuable lessons for future success.

By practicing these techniques, individuals can overcome their fears and doubts about their financial future and move towards financial success. Remember that it takes time and effort to change limiting beliefs and overcome negative emotions, but the rewards of financial freedom and security are worth the effort.

In conclusion, cultivating a wealth mindset is crucial for achieving financial success. It involves developing positive attitudes toward wealth and success, setting effective goals, and taking action while holding oneself accountable. Limiting beliefs and negative thoughts must be identified and challenged to be replaced with empowering beliefs. By reframing negative beliefs and replacing them with positive ones, one can overcome fear and doubt about their financial future. It takes effort, commitment, and consistency to cultivate a wealth mindset, but the benefits are significant and long-lasting. With a wealth mindset, anyone can achieve financial success and live the life they desire.

Chapter 7

7.1 The Connection Between Self-Worth and Financial Success

The connection between self-worth and financial success is a complex and often overlooked aspect of personal finance. It is commonly believed that financial success is solely determined by external factors such as education, skill set, and market trends. However, recent studies have shown that a person's sense of self-worth and self-esteem play a significant role in their ability to achieve financial success.

Self-worth can be defined as a person's belief in their own value and worth as an individual. This belief can be influenced by factors such as upbringing, life experiences, and social conditioning. When it comes to finances, a person's sense of self-worth can impact their financial decision-making, income, and wealth accumulation.

Individuals with a high sense of self-worth tend to make more confident financial decisions, take calculated risks, and negotiate higher salaries or fees. They also tend to have a greater ability to bounce back from financial setbacks and learn from their mistakes. This confidence and resilience can lead to greater financial success over time.

On the other hand, individuals with a low sense of self-worth may struggle with financial decision-making and find it difficult to advocate for themselves in negotiations. They may also experience self-doubt and anxiety around money, which can lead to avoiding financial decisions or making decisions based on fear rather than logic.

It is important to note that self-worth is not synonymous with net worth. A person's financial situation does not necessarily reflect their value as a person. However, a person's sense of self-worth can impact their financial behavior and the outcomes they achieve.

So how can one improve their self-worth and in turn, their financial success? Here are some strategies to consider:

7.2 Identify and challenge negative self-talk:

Negative self-talk can be detrimental to both self-worth and financial success. Identifying and challenging negative self-talk can help improve confidence and decision-making.

7.3 Practice self-care:

Prioritizing self-care activities such as exercise, sleep, and meditation can improve overall well-being and lead to greater confidence and resilience.

7.4 Surround yourself with positive influences:

The people we surround ourselves with can impact our sense of self-worth. Surrounding oneself with positive and supportive individuals can improve self-esteem and confidence.

7.5 Celebrate accomplishments:

Celebrating accomplishments, no matter how small, can help build confidence and a sense of pride in one's abilities.

7.6 Seek professional help:

For individuals struggling with low self-worth, seeking the help of a therapist or counselor can be beneficial.

In conclusion, there is a strong connection between self-worth and financial success. Your self-worth and self-esteem impact your thoughts, beliefs, and actions, which can ultimately determine your financial success. Negative self-talk, limiting beliefs, and low self-esteem can hold you back from taking risks, pursuing opportunities, and achieving your financial goals.

It's important to recognize and challenge any negative self-talk or limiting beliefs you may have about money and wealth. By reframing these beliefs and adopting a wealth mindset, you can develop a more positive and empowering perspective that will help you take action towards your financial goals.

Additionally, setting specific, measurable goals and creating a plan for achieving them can help you stay motivated and accountable. Measuring your progress and celebrating your successes can also help build your confidence and reinforce your sense of self-worth.

It's also crucial to remember that financial success is not the only measure of self-worth. It's important to prioritize your mental, emotional, and physical well-being, as well as your relationships and personal fulfillment. By nurturing a healthy sense of self-worth, you can create a more balanced and fulfilling life overall.

Chapter 8

8.1 Practicing Positive Self-Talk to Support Your Wealth Mindset

Practicing Positive Self-Talk to Support Your Wealth Mindset Practicing positive self-talk is a powerful tool that can help you support and strengthen your wealth mindset. The way we talk to ourselves has a significant impact on our beliefs, actions, and ultimately, our financial success. When we use negative self-talk, we create a self-fulfilling prophecy that reinforces limiting beliefs and undermines our confidence in our abilities.

Positive self-talk, on the other hand, can help us cultivate a growth mindset and develop a more empowering relationship with money and wealth. By focusing on our strengths, accomplishments, and potential, we can overcome self-doubt and fear and tap into our inner resources to achieve our financial goals.

Here are some strategies for practicing positive self-talk to support your wealth mindset:

8.2 Identify your negative self-talk patterns:

The first step in practicing positive self-talk is to become aware of your negative self-talk patterns. Pay attention to the thoughts and beliefs that are holding you back, such as "I'm not good with money" or "I'll never be wealthy." Write them down and challenge them with positive, empowering statements.

8.3 Replace negative self-talk with positive affirmations:

Once you've identified your negative self-talk patterns, replace them with positive affirmations. For example, instead of saying "I'm bad with money," say "I'm learning to manage my finances effectively." Repeat these affirmations to yourself daily, preferably in front of a mirror.

8.4 Focus on your strengths and accomplishments:

To build confidence in your abilities, focus on your strengths and accomplishments. Make a list of your skills, talents, and achievements, and remind yourself of them often. Celebrate your successes, no matter how small they may seem.

8.5 Visualize your success:

Visualization is a powerful technique for manifesting your desires and goals. Spend a few minutes each day visualizing yourself achieving your financial goals. Imagine the feeling of accomplishment and success, and let yourself feel the emotions associated with that success.

8.6 Surround yourself with positivity:

Surround yourself with positive influences, such as supportive friends and family, inspiring books, podcasts, and videos, and uplifting affirmations. Avoid negative news, gossip, and toxic people that drain your energy and undermine your confidence.

In conclusion, practicing positive self-talk is an essential part of cultivating a wealth mindset. By replacing negative self-talk with empowering affirmations, focusing on your strengths and accomplishments, visualizing your success, and surrounding yourself with positivity, you can overcome self-doubt and fear and tap into your inner resources to achieve your financial goals. Remember, the way you talk to yourself matters, so choose your words wisely and believe in your ability to create the financial future you desire.

Chapter 9

9.1 The Role of Visualization in Overcoming Limiting Beliefs

Visualization is a powerful technique that can help you overcome limiting beliefs and achieve your financial goals. Visualization involves using your imagination to create mental images of the outcomes you want to achieve in your life.

When it comes to financial success, visualization can be an effective tool to help you overcome limiting beliefs about money and wealth. For example, if you have a belief that you are not worthy of financial success, you may find it difficult to take the necessary steps to achieve your goals. Visualization can help you overcome this limiting belief by allowing you to see yourself as someone who is capable of achieving financial success.

To practice visualization, find a quiet and comfortable place where you can relax and focus your mind. Close your eyes and take several deep breaths to help you relax. Then, create a mental image of the outcome you want to achieve. For example, if your goal is to earn a certain amount of money, visualize yourself receiving a check for that amount or seeing the balance in your bank account increase by that amount.

As you visualize, use all of your senses to create a vivid and realistic mental image. Imagine the sights, sounds, smells, and sensations associated with achieving your goal. Feel the excitement and satisfaction of accomplishing what you set out to do.

It's important to note that visualization alone is not enough to achieve your financial goals. You must also take action and make a plan to achieve your goals. Visualization can help you stay motivated and focused on your goals, but it's up to you to take the necessary steps to make them a reality.

In addition to visualization, there are other techniques you can use to overcome limiting beliefs and achieve financial success. These include positive affirmations, meditation, and seeking support from a coach or mentor. By combining these techniques with visualization, you can develop a powerful mindset that supports your financial success.

I can provide an explanation of the role of visualization in overcoming limiting beliefs in point form:

- Visualization is the process of creating mental images or scenarios of desired outcomes in your mind.
- By visualizing yourself achieving your goals and overcoming obstacles, you can train your brain to focus on positive outcomes and reprogram negative thought patterns.
- Visualization can help you overcome limiting beliefs by creating a new mental image of

yourself as someone who is capable of achieving financial success.

- Visualization can also help you develop a clear and detailed vision of your financial goals, which can help you stay motivated and focused.
- To use visualization effectively, it's important to find a quiet space where you can focus your mind and visualize your goals in detail.
- Visualization can be combined with other techniques such as affirmations, goal-setting, and meditation to create a powerful mindset shift towards financial success.
- Visualization can also help you develop a sense of emotional attachment to your goals, which can help you stay motivated and persistent in the face of obstacles.
- Visualization can be used in various aspects of financial planning, such as envisioning yourself earning a certain income, saving a certain amount of money, or paying off debt.
- By consistently practicing visualization techniques, you can gradually shift your mindset and overcome limiting beliefs about your financial abilities.
- Visualization is a powerful tool that can help you create a clear and compelling vision of your financial future, and stay motivated and focused on your goals.

In conclusion visualization can be a powerful tool in overcoming limiting beliefs and achieving financial success. By visualizing your goals and the steps you need to take to achieve them, you can create a clear mental picture of what you want and stay motivated to work towards it. Additionally, visualization can help to reprogram your subconscious mind and replace limiting beliefs with positive, empowering thoughts. Overall, incorporating visualization into your mindset and goal-setting strategies can help you to overcome obstacles and achieve financial success.

Chapter 10

10.1 Strategies for Maintaining a Positive Mindset Even When Facing Challenges

Maintaining a positive mindset is essential for achieving success in any area of life, including financial success. While it can be challenging to remain positive when facing setbacks and challenges, there are several strategies that can help:

10.2 Reframe negative situations:

Instead of seeing setbacks and failures as signs of defeat, view them as opportunities to learn and grow. Focus on the lessons you can take away from the experience rather than dwelling on the negative aspects.

10.3 Practice gratitude:

Gratitude is a powerful tool for maintaining a positive mindset. Take time each day to reflect on the things you are grateful for, even if they are small. This can help shift your focus away from the negative and towards the positive.

10.4 Surround yourself with positivity:

The people and environments we surround ourselves with can have a significant impact on our mindset. Seek out positive people and uplifting environments that support your goals and values.

10.5 Set realistic expectations:

Unrealistic expectations can lead to disappointment and a negative mindset. Set goals that are challenging yet achievable, and celebrate each step of progress towards achieving them.

10.6 Take care of yourself:

Physical and mental health can greatly impact our mindset. Take care of yourself by eating well, exercising regularly, and practicing self-care activities that bring you joy and relaxation.

10.7 Focus on the Positive:

Instead of dwelling on the negatives, try to focus on the positives. Look for opportunities to learn from setbacks and challenges, and focus on the progress you have made rather than the distance left to go. When you focus on the positive, you are more likely to stay motivated and optimistic.

10.8 Surround Yourself with Positivity:

Surrounding yourself with positivity can help you maintain a positive mindset. Spend time with people who uplift and inspire you, and limit your exposure to negative influences, whether it be negative news, negative people, or negative self-talk.

10.9 Practice Self-Care:

Taking care of yourself is essential for maintaining a positive mindset. Make time for activities that bring you joy and relaxation, such as exercise, meditation, or hobbies. When you feel good physically and emotionally, you are more likely to maintain a positive mindset.

10.10 Use Affirmations:

Affirmations are powerful statements that can help you maintain a positive mindset. Choose affirmations that resonate with you, and repeat them to yourself daily. Affirmations can help you reprogram your subconscious mind, replacing negative self-talk with positive, empowering beliefs.

10.11 Keep a Positive Perspective:

Keeping a positive perspective can help you maintain a positive mindset, even in the face of challenges. Instead of seeing obstacles as insurmountable barriers, see them as opportunities to learn and grow. Remember that setbacks are temporary, and that you have the strength and resilience to overcome them.

By implementing these strategies, you can maintain a positive mindset even when facing challenges and setbacks on your path towards financial success. Remember to focus on the lessons you can learn from each experience, practice gratitude, surround yourself with positivity, set realistic expectations, and take care of yourself both physically and mentally.

In conclusion, maintaining a positive mindset is critical for achieving financial success, especially during challenging times. By using various strategies such as staying focused on your goals, practicing gratitude, and seeking support from others, you can cultivate a resilient mindset that allows you to overcome obstacles and stay on track toward achieving your financial objectives. It is important to remember that setbacks and challenges are a normal part of the journey, and a positive mindset can help you see them as opportunities for growth and learning. By staying committed to your goals and staying positive, you can achieve financial success and enjoy a fulfilling life.

Part 3 Complete

Part 4

Taking Action

A wealth mindset is not just about thinking differently, it's also about taking action. In this part, you'll learn strategies for taking consistent, intentional action toward their financial goals. It will provide tips for staying motivated and overcoming obstacles along the way.

Chapter 1

1.1 The Importance of Taking Consistent Action Toward Your Financial Goals

Taking consistent action is critical to achieving financial goals. No matter how great your goals are, they won't come to fruition if you don't take action to make them happen. Whether it's building an emergency fund, saving for retirement, or paying off debt, consistent action is the key to success.

Consistency is important because it creates momentum. When you take small steps toward your goals each day, you build momentum that can carry you forward, even when things get tough. It's like pushing a boulder up a hill: it may be difficult at first, but once you get it rolling, it becomes easier to keep going.

To maintain consistency, it's important to set achievable goals and break them down into smaller, manageable steps. This helps you avoid feeling overwhelmed and keeps you motivated. It's also important to create a plan and schedule regular check-ins to evaluate your progress and make any necessary adjustments.

Another key to taking consistent action is to establish healthy habits. Habits are the things we do automatically without having to think about them. When you establish healthy habits, like automatically saving a percentage of your income or reviewing your budget regularly, you remove the need to rely on willpower to take action.

Consistent action requires discipline, commitment, and a willingness to prioritize your goals over short-term pleasures. It's not always easy, but the rewards are worth it. When you take consistent action toward your financial goals, you'll build a sense of confidence and empowerment that can carry over into other areas of your life.

Taking consistent action towards your financial goals is crucial for achieving long-term success. Here are some reasons why:

1.2 Builds momentum:
When you consistently take action towards your financial goals, you build momentum and create a sense of progress, which can motivate you to keep going.

1.3 Helps overcome obstacles:

Consistent action can help you overcome obstacles and challenges that arise along the way. By taking action, you can identify problems and find solutions.

1.4 Creates habits:

Consistent action can help you create positive habits that support your financial goals. Over time, these habits can become automatic, making it easier to achieve your goals.

1.5 Increases focus:

Taking consistent action can help you stay focused on your goals and avoid distractions that could derail your progress.

1.6 Builds confidence:

Consistent action can help you build confidence in your ability to achieve your goals, which can lead to increased motivation and success.

In conclusion, taking consistent action is crucial for achieving financial success. By setting achievable goals, breaking them down into smaller steps, establishing healthy habits, and maintaining discipline and commitment, you can build momentum and achieve your financial goals over time. Remember, small actions done consistently can lead to big results.

Chapter 2

2.1 Overcoming Procrastination and Taking Action Now

Procrastination is a common challenge that many people face when it comes to taking action towards their financial goals. It is the tendency to delay or postpone tasks, even when you know they are important or necessary. Overcoming procrastination is essential for achieving financial success, as taking consistent action is critical in reaching your goals. In this section, we will explore some strategies for overcoming procrastination and taking action now.

2.2 Recognize the problem:

The first step in overcoming procrastination is to recognize that it is a problem. Admitting that you have a tendency to procrastinate is the first step towards addressing the issue. Take some time to reflect on your habits and behaviors and identify areas where you tend to procrastinate the most.

2.3 Set clear goals:

Setting clear goals is essential for overcoming procrastination. When you have a specific goal in mind, it becomes easier to focus and prioritize your actions. Make sure your goals are specific, measurable, and time-bound, and break them down into smaller, manageable tasks.

2.4 Create a plan:

Once you have set clear goals, create a plan of action. Identify the steps you need to take to achieve your goals and establish a timeline for completing each task. Break down each task into smaller, more manageable steps and prioritize them according to their level of importance.

2.5 Remove distractions:

Distractions can be a significant cause of procrastination. To overcome this, create an environment that is conducive to work. Remove any distractions such as social media notifications, email notifications, or other distractions that can take away your focus.

2.6 Use the Pomodoro Technique:

The Pomodoro Technique is a time management method that can help you overcome procrastination. It involves working in short, focused bursts of 25 minutes, followed by a short break. This method helps you to stay focused and avoid distractions.

2.7 Hold yourself accountable:

Holding yourself accountable is critical for overcoming procrastination. Find ways to hold yourself accountable, such as setting deadlines for completing tasks or tracking your progress towards your goals. You can also enlist the help of an accountability partner or coach to help you stay on track.

2.8 Celebrate your progress:

Celebrating your progress can help you to stay motivated and overcome procrastination. Whenever you complete a task or achieve a milestone, take the time to acknowledge your progress and celebrate your achievements. This will help you to stay positive and focused on your goals.

In conclusion, overcoming procrastination is essential for taking consistent action towards your financial goals. By recognizing the problem, setting clear goals, creating a plan, removing distractions, using the Pomodoro technique, holding yourself accountable, and celebrating your progress, you can overcome procrastination and take action now.

Chapter 3

3.1 Strategies for Prioritizing Your Actions and Time

Strategies for prioritizing your actions and time involve organizing your tasks in a way that aligns with your goals and values. This includes identifying which tasks are most important and urgent and scheduling them accordingly. It also involves learning to say no to tasks that do not align with your priorities and delegating tasks when possible. Additionally, taking breaks and practicing self-care can help increase productivity and focus. Overall, prioritizing your actions and time requires a clear understanding of your goals and values, effective time management, and the ability to make intentional choices about how to spend your time.

Prioritizing your actions and time is essential for achieving your financial goals. With limited time and resources, it's important to focus on the most important tasks that will bring you closer to your desired outcome. Here are some strategies for prioritizing your actions and time:

3.2 Set Clear Goals:

Before you can prioritize your actions and time, you need to know what you're working towards. Set clear and specific financial goals that align with your values and vision for the future. This will help you stay focused and motivated, and will make it easier to prioritize your actions.

3.3 Identify Urgent vs. Important Tasks:

Not all tasks are created equal. Some tasks may be urgent but not important, while others may be important but not urgent. Identify the tasks that are both urgent and important, and prioritize those first. This will help you avoid getting sidetracked by less important tasks.

3.4 Use a To-Do List:

A to-do list is a great way to keep track of all the tasks you need to accomplish. Write down everything you need to do, and then prioritize the tasks in order of importance. This will help you stay organized and focused, and will ensure that you don't forget anything important.

3.5 Break Down Big Tasks:

Big tasks can be overwhelming, which can make it difficult to prioritize them. To make it easier, break big tasks down into smaller, more manageable tasks. This will make it easier to prioritize the individual steps, and will help you make progress towards your goal.

3.6 Learn to Say No:

Saying no can be difficult, especially when it comes to work or social commitments. However, it's important to prioritize your time and energy. If a task or commitment isn't aligned with your goals or values, it may be better to say no and focus on what's truly important.

3.7 Use Time-Blocking:

Time-blocking is a technique that involves scheduling blocks of time for specific tasks. This can help you stay focused and avoid distractions, and can also help you make progress towards your goals. Block off time for your most important tasks first, and then schedule other tasks around them.

3.8 Review and Adjust:

Priorities can change over time, so it's important to review and adjust your priorities regularly. Take a look at your to-do list and schedule, and make sure that you're still focused on the most important tasks. If something isn't working, don't be afraid to adjust your priorities and schedule.

By prioritizing your actions and time, you can ensure that you're making progress towards your financial goals. These strategies can help you stay focused and motivated, and can help you overcome obstacles and challenges along the way.

Chapter 4

4.1 The Benefits of Creating Daily Rituals and Routines

Creating daily rituals and routines can have numerous benefits for individuals looking to achieve financial success. By incorporating consistent habits into their daily lives, individuals can develop a sense of structure and organization, which can help them stay focused and motivated.

Creating daily rituals and routines can have significant benefits for individuals who are working towards achieving their financial goals. Here are some strategies that can be helpful:

4.2 Consistency:

One of the primary benefits of creating daily rituals and routines is that it provides consistency in your actions. When you make your goals a part of your daily routine, you are more likely to stick to them and see progress over time.

4.3 Accountability:

Creating daily rituals and routines can also help you hold yourself accountable for your actions. By setting specific times to work on your financial goals, you are making a commitment to yourself and increasing the likelihood of following through.

4.4 Time management:

Daily rituals and routines can help you manage your time more effectively. By prioritizing your actions and scheduling them into your day, you can make the most of your time and ensure that you are making progress towards your financial goals.

4.5 Stress reduction:

Having a daily routine can also help reduce stress and increase overall well-being. When you have a plan in place, you can feel more in control and confident in your ability to achieve your goals.

4.6 Building habits:

Creating daily rituals and routines can help you build new habits that support your financial goals. Over time, these habits can become automatic and ingrained in your daily routine, making it easier to achieve long-term success.

To create daily rituals and routines that support your financial goals, consider the following:

4.7 Identify your goals:

Start by identifying your financial goals and the specific actions you need to take to achieve them.

4.8 Prioritize your actions:

Determine which actions are most important and prioritize them in your daily routine.

4.9 Schedule your day:

Block out specific times in your day to work on your financial goals, and be sure to stick to your schedule.

4.10 Build in flexibility:

While consistency is important, it is also important to build in flexibility to your routine. Life happens, and unexpected events can come up, so be prepared to adjust your routine as needed.

4.11 Track your progress:

Regularly track your progress towards your financial goals. This can help you stay motivated and adjust your routine as needed to continue making progress.

Overall, creating daily rituals and routines can be an effective strategy for achieving your financial goals. By providing consistency, accountability, time management, stress reduction, and habit building, daily rituals and routines can help you make progress towards your financial goals and improve your overall well-being.

Having daily rituals and routines can also increase efficiency and productivity by streamlining tasks and minimizing decision-making. When certain tasks become automatic, it frees up mental space and energy to tackle other important responsibilities.

In addition, daily rituals and routines can help reduce stress and anxiety by providing a sense of stability and predictability. This can be especially important when dealing with financial stressors, as it can help individuals feel more in control of their situation.

In conclusion, creating daily rituals and routines can be a powerful tool in achieving financial success. By incorporating positive habits and behaviors into your daily life, you can create a sense of structure and consistency that can help you stay focused on your goals. These habits can help you manage your time more effectively, increase your productivity, and build a strong foundation for success. By making small changes to your daily routine, you can make a big impact on your financial future. So, take the time to identify the habits that will help you achieve your goals, and commit to incorporating them into your daily routine. With consistency and dedication, you can create the life and financial success that you desire.

Chapter 5

5.1 How to Stay Motivated and Focused on Your Financial Goals

To stay motivated and focused on your financial goals, you need to have a clear understanding of your "why." Why do you want to achieve these goals? What is the underlying motivation behind your desire for financial success? This can be anything from providing a better life for your family to achieving financial freedom and security.

Once you have identified your "why," it is important to break down your goals into smaller, achievable steps. This will help you avoid feeling overwhelmed or discouraged by the size of the task ahead. Make sure to celebrate your progress along the way, no matter how small.

Another key factor in staying motivated and focused is accountability. Share your goals with others and ask them to hold you accountable. Consider working with a financial advisor or coach who can provide guidance and support along the way.

Staying motivated and focused on your financial goals can be a challenging task, especially when faced with setbacks and distractions. However, maintaining a positive attitude and a clear vision of your goals can help you stay on track and achieve financial success. Here are some strategies to help you stay motivated and focused on your financial goals:

5.2 Create a clear and specific plan:

Having a well-defined plan is crucial for staying focused and motivated. Write down your financial goals and the specific steps you need to take to achieve them. Make sure your plan is realistic and achievable, but also challenging enough to keep you motivated.

5.3 Break your goals into smaller tasks:

Sometimes, the thought of tackling a big project can be overwhelming, and it's easy to get discouraged. To avoid this, break down your financial goals into smaller, more manageable tasks. This will help you stay motivated and focused by allowing you to see progress towards your goals.

5.4 Celebrate small wins:

Celebrating small wins along the way can help you stay motivated and focused on your financial goals. This can be as simple as treating yourself to a nice meal or a small purchase once you've reached a milestone.

5.5 Surround yourself with positive influences:

Surrounding yourself with people who are supportive of your goals can help you stay motivated and focused. Seek out people who are also working towards similar financial goals or who have already achieved them. Joining a support group or finding a mentor can also be helpful.

5.6 Use visualization techniques:

Visualizing yourself achieving your financial goals can help you stay motivated and focused. Take time each day to imagine yourself living the life you want to live and experiencing the rewards of achieving your goals. This can help keep you motivated and focused on your goals.

5.7 Stay organized:

Being organized can help you stay focused and motivated. Keep track of your progress towards your financial goals by using a planner, spreadsheet, or other organizational tools. This will help you stay on top of your tasks and prevent you from getting sidetracked.

5.8 Learn from setbacks:

Setbacks are a natural part of the journey towards achieving financial goals. Instead of getting discouraged, use setbacks as an opportunity to learn and grow. Analyze what went wrong and what you can do differently next time to prevent the same mistake.

Finally, make sure to take care of yourself both mentally and physically. This includes getting enough sleep, eating well, and engaging in activities that bring you joy and relaxation. A healthy mind and body will help you stay energized and focused on achieving your financial goals.

In conclusion, staying motivated and focused on your financial goals requires a combination of discipline, positive thinking, and effective planning. By implementing these strategies, you can stay on track and achieve financial success.

Chapter 6

6.1 Coping with Setbacks and Obstacles Along the Way

Achieving financial goals is rarely a smooth and uninterrupted journey. Setbacks and obstacles are inevitable, and they can easily derail our efforts and dampen our motivation. Therefore, it is important to develop strategies for coping with setbacks and obstacles along the way. Here are some tips to help you stay on track:

6.2 Accept the reality of setbacks:

It is natural to feel disappointed or frustrated when things do not go as planned. However, it is important to accept that setbacks and obstacles are a normal part of the journey towards financial success. By acknowledging this fact, you can better prepare yourself to handle them when they arise.

6.3 Reframe setbacks as opportunities for growth:

Instead of viewing setbacks as failures, try to see them as opportunities for learning and growth. Each setback provides valuable feedback that can help you refine your approach and improve your strategies.

6.4 Stay focused on your long-term goals:

Setbacks can be demotivating, but it is important to keep your eyes on the prize. Stay focused on your long-term financial goals, and remind yourself of the reasons why you started on this journey in the first place.

6.5 Take a break if you need to:

Sometimes, the best thing you can do when facing a setback or obstacle is to take a break. This can give you time to regroup, refocus, and come up with a new plan of action.

6.6 Seek support from others:

It can be helpful to seek support from friends, family members, or a financial advisor when facing setbacks. They can provide a fresh perspective, offer encouragement, and help you brainstorm new ideas.

6.7 Practice self-care:

Setbacks can be emotionally taxing, so it is important to take care of yourself during these times. This may include getting enough sleep, eating healthy foods, exercising regularly, and engaging in activities that bring you joy and relaxation.

6.8 Learn from your mistakes:

When setbacks occur, it is important to reflect on what went wrong and what you could do differently in the future. Use the experience as an opportunity to learn and grow, rather than dwelling on the past. By implementing these strategies, you can better cope with setbacks and obstacles along the way to achieving your financial goals. Remember that setbacks are temporary, and with perseverance and a positive attitude, you can overcome them and continue on your path towards financial success. Some more factors are:

6.9 Stay positive:

When you face setbacks and obstacles, it's easy to get discouraged and feel like giving up. However, it's important to stay positive and keep your mindset focused on your goals. You can do this by focusing on the progress you've already made, reminding yourself of your strengths and capabilities, and staying connected to your "why" or motivation for pursuing your financial goals.

6.10 Learn from your setbacks:

Setbacks can be valuable learning opportunities. Take the time to reflect on what went wrong, what you could have done differently, and what you can learn from the experience. Use this information to adjust your strategy and approach moving forward.

6.11 Break down your goals into smaller steps:

Sometimes, setbacks and obstacles can feel overwhelming when you're looking at the big picture. By breaking down your financial goals into smaller, more manageable steps, you can make progress towards your goals and stay motivated.

6.12 Stay accountable:

Having someone to hold you accountable can be a powerful motivator. This could be a friend, family member, or financial advisor. By checking in regularly with someone who supports your goals, you can stay on track and motivated.

6.13 Take action:

Sometimes the best way to deal with setbacks and obstacles is to take action. This could mean adjusting your budget, seeking out new income opportunities, or finding ways to reduce expenses. By taking action, you can regain a sense of control and momentum towards your goals.

6.14 Practice self-care:

Pursuing financial goals can be stressful, so it's important to take care of yourself along the way. This could mean taking breaks when you need them, seeking out support from friends and family, or engaging in activities that bring you joy and relaxation.

In summary, coping with setbacks and obstacles when pursuing financial goals requires a combination of mindset, strategy, and self-care. By staying positive, learning from setbacks, breaking down goals into smaller steps, staying accountable, taking action, and practicing self-care, you can overcome obstacles and stay motivated towards achieving your financial goals.

Chapter 7

7.1 The Power of Learning from Failure and Mistakes

The power of learning from failure and mistakes is an essential aspect of achieving success in any area of life, including finances. Failure and mistakes are often viewed negatively, but they can be valuable opportunities for growth and learning. When we make mistakes or experience failures, we have a chance to reflect on what went wrong and identify areas for improvement.

Learning from failure and mistakes involves a process of self-reflection and analysis. It requires us to be honest with ourselves about what happened and why it happened. It is essential to take responsibility for our mistakes and not to blame others for our failures. When we accept responsibility, we can learn from our mistakes and avoid repeating them in the future.

One of the most significant benefits of learning from failure and mistakes is that it can lead to innovation and creativity. When we try new things, we may make mistakes, but those mistakes can lead to new ideas and ways of doing things. By learning from our mistakes, we can improve our processes and develop new strategies to achieve our goals.

Learning from failure and mistakes also helps us develop resilience. Resilience is the ability to bounce back from setbacks and challenges. When we experience failure or make mistakes, it can be discouraging and demotivating. However, if we can learn from those experiences and use them to grow, we become more resilient and better equipped to handle future challenges.

One of the keys to learning from failure and mistakes is to have a growth mindset. A growth mindset is the belief that our abilities and intelligence can be developed through dedication and hard work. When we have a growth mindset, we view failure and mistakes as opportunities for growth and improvement, rather than as signs of incompetence or lack of ability.

To learn from failure and mistakes, it is important to take time to reflect on what happened and why. Ask yourself questions like: What went wrong? What could I have done differently? What did I learn from this experience? It is also helpful to seek feedback from others, especially from those who have experience in the area where you experienced failure or made a mistake.

Another important aspect of learning from failure and mistakes is to take action based on what you have learned. It is not enough to reflect on what happened; you also need to take steps to improve and make changes. This may involve developing new skills, changing your approach or mindset, or seeking help from others.

It is also important to recognize that learning from failure and mistakes is a continuous process. We will never be perfect, and we will always make mistakes. However, by continually learning from our experiences and using that knowledge to improve, we can become more effective and successful in our financial endeavors.

In conclusion, the power of learning from failure and mistakes cannot be overstated. By embracing failure and mistakes as opportunities for growth and improvement, we can become more resilient, creative, and successful. To learn from failure and mistakes, we need to have a growth mindset, take time to reflect on our experiences, seek feedback, and take action based on what we have learned.

Chapter 8

8.1 The Connection Between Risk-Taking and Financial Success

The connection between risk-taking and financial success is a well-established concept. To achieve financial success, one must be willing to take risks, which often involves stepping out of one's comfort zone and into the unknown. While taking risks can be intimidating and may lead to failure, it is essential for growth and development in both personal and professional spheres.

Here are some key points to understand the connection between risk-taking and financial success:

- Risk-taking is a necessary step towards achieving financial success. Taking calculated risks, such as investing in the stock market or starting a business, can lead to higher returns and financial rewards. However, it is important to note that not all risks are created equal, and one must weigh the potential benefits against the potential drawbacks.

- Successful risk-takers often have a high tolerance for uncertainty and ambiguity. They are comfortable with the idea of not knowing what the future holds and are willing to take a chance on their ideas or investments. This mindset allows them to embrace uncertainty and view it as an opportunity for growth.

- Risk-taking is not synonymous with recklessness. While taking risks is essential for financial success, it is important to approach it in a measured and strategic way. Successful risk-takers evaluate their options, gather information, and make informed decisions based on the available data. They also have contingency plans in place in case their risks do not pan out as expected.

- Failure is often a necessary part of the risk-taking process. While failure can be discouraging, it is essential for growth and development. Successful risk-takers view failure as a learning opportunity and use it to refine their approach and strategy.

- The willingness to take risks is often a key differentiator between those who achieve financial success and those who do not. Many successful entrepreneurs and investors credit their success to taking calculated risks and being willing to step out of their comfort zones.

Here are some additional points to consider when exploring the connection between risk-taking and financial success:

8.2 Risk-taking is a key element of entrepreneurship:

Many successful entrepreneurs attribute their success to their willingness to take risks. When starting a business, entrepreneurs take a risk by investing their time, money, and resources into an idea that may or may not succeed. Without this willingness to take a chance, many businesses would never get off the ground.

8.3 Risk-taking can lead to greater rewards:

When it comes to investing, the potential for greater returns often comes with a higher level of risk. Investments with high potential returns, such as stocks or real estate, also come with a greater risk of loss. However, for those who are willing to take on this risk, the rewards can be substantial.

8.4 Risk-taking requires a careful balance:

While taking risks can be beneficial, it's important to find a balance between taking risks and being cautious. Too much risk can lead to financial ruin, while too little risk can lead to missed opportunities for growth and success. Finding the right balance requires careful planning, research, and evaluation of potential risks and rewards.

8.5 Risk-taking is not the same as being reckless:

It's important to note that taking risks does not mean being reckless with your finances. Careful evaluation of risks and rewards, as well as taking steps to minimize risk, are important components of responsible risk-taking.

8.6 Calculated risk-taking can lead to financial growth:

Taking calculated risks, such as investing in a well-researched stock or starting a business after careful planning and evaluation, can lead to significant financial growth. By weighing the potential risks and rewards and taking steps to minimize risk, individuals can increase their chances of success and achieve their financial goals.

8.7 Risk-taking requires a long-term perspective:

Taking risks in the pursuit of financial success often requires a long-term perspective. While some risks may pay off quickly, others may take time to yield results. It's important to be patient and persistent, and to maintain a focus on long-term goals when taking risks.

8.8 Risk-taking can build confidence:

Successfully taking risks and achieving financial success can also help to build confidence and self-esteem. This can lead to greater willingness to take on new challenges and pursue even greater opportunities for growth and success.

In conclusion, risk-taking can be a powerful tool for achieving financial success. By carefully evaluating risks and rewards, finding the right balance between caution and risk-taking, and maintaining a long-term perspective, individuals can increase their chances of success and achieve their financial goals. However, it's important to remember that responsible risk-taking requires careful planning and evaluation, and is not the same as being reckless with your finances.

Chapter 9

9.1 The Importance of Flexibility and Adaptability in Pursuing Your Goals

Flexibility and adaptability are essential qualities for anyone pursuing their financial goals. As much as we may plan and prepare, life is unpredictable, and unexpected events can arise at any time. These events can significantly impact our progress towards our financial goals, and without flexibility and adaptability, we may become discouraged and lose momentum.

Flexibility means being able to change our plans as needed to accommodate new circumstances. It means being open to new opportunities and ideas that may present themselves and adjusting our approach accordingly. This can involve re-evaluating our goals and priorities or modifying our strategies to better align with our current situation.

Adaptability refers to our ability to respond effectively to changing circumstances. It involves being resilient in the face of challenges and setbacks and finding ways to overcome them. It means being able to adjust our mindset and behavior to better handle the challenges we encounter along the way.

There are several strategies that can help us develop flexibility and adaptability in pursuing our financial goals:

9.2 Embrace change:

Recognize that change is a natural part of life and that we must adapt to new circumstances as they arise. We can develop this mindset by being open to new experiences, trying new things, and stepping outside of our comfort zone.

9.3 Maintain a growth mindset:

Adopting a growth mindset means believing that our abilities and qualities can be developed through hard work and dedication. By cultivating this mindset, we can approach challenges as opportunities for growth and development rather than insurmountable obstacles.

9.4 Be willing to pivot:

Sometimes, our initial plans may not work out as we anticipated. In these cases, it is essential to be willing to pivot and change our approach. This could involve modifying our goals or strategies, seeking out new opportunities, or changing our mindset to better handle the challenges we encounter.

9.5 Stay focused on the big picture:

While it is important to be flexible and adaptable, it is also essential to keep our long-term goals in mind. By staying focused on the big picture, we can maintain our motivation and momentum even in the face of setbacks and challenges.

9.6 Practice mindfulness:

Mindfulness involves being present in the moment and paying attention to our thoughts, feelings, and surroundings. By practicing mindfulness, we can become more aware of our emotions and better equipped to manage them in the face of unexpected events.

To become more flexible and adaptable in pursuit of your financial goals, you can take the following steps:

9.7 Keep an Open Mind:

Be open to new ideas, perspectives, and approaches. Don't be afraid to challenge your assumptions and be willing to learn from others.

9.8 Be Willing to Experiment:

Don't be afraid to try new things and experiment with different approaches. You never know what may work until you try it.

9.9 Embrace Change:

Instead of resisting change, try to embrace it. Be willing to adapt your plans and approach as circumstances change.

9.10 Continuously Learn and Improve:

Stay up-to-date with industry trends and new technologies, and invest in your education and personal development. The more you know, the better equipped you will be to adapt to new situations.

9.11 Network and Collaborate:

Build a network of contacts and collaborators who can offer support and guidance. Collaborating with others can bring new ideas and opportunities to light and help you stay flexible and adaptable in pursuit of your goals.

In summary, flexibility and adaptability are crucial qualities for anyone pursuing their financial goals. By embracing change, maintaining a growth mindset, being willing to pivot, staying focused on the big picture, and practicing mindfulness, we can develop these qualities and navigate the challenges that arise along the way.

Chapter 10

10.1 Celebrating Your Successes and Progress Along the Way

Celebrating your successes and progress along the way is a critical part of achieving financial success. It is important to recognize and acknowledge your accomplishments, no matter how small they may seem. Celebrating your successes not only helps you maintain a positive attitude and stay motivated, but it also provides you with the energy and confidence you need to keep moving forward.

Here are some reasons why celebrating your successes and progress is so important:

10.2 Boosts morale:

Celebrating your successes and progress boosts your morale and creates a positive feedback loop. When you take time to appreciate your accomplishments, you feel good about yourself and your abilities. This positive feeling can then fuel your motivation to continue working towards your goals.

10.3 Provides motivation:

Celebrating your successes and progress can provide you with the motivation you need to keep going. When you feel like you are making progress, you are more likely to continue working towards your goals. Celebrating your successes also reminds you of the progress you have made and helps you stay focused on your long-term goals.

10.4 Reinforces positive behavior:

Celebrating your successes and progress reinforces positive behavior. When you take time to acknowledge your accomplishments, you are more likely to continue doing the things that got you there in the first place. This reinforces positive habits and behaviors, making it more likely that you will achieve your financial goals.

10.5 Helps build resilience:

Celebrating your successes and progress can help you build resilience. When you experience setbacks or failures, it can be easy to become discouraged and lose motivation. However, if you have taken the time to celebrate your successes along the way, you have a reserve of positive feelings and experiences to draw upon. This can help you bounce back more quickly and stay focused on your long-term goals.

So how can you celebrate your successes and progress along the way? Here are some ideas:

10.6 Reflect on your accomplishments:

Take time to reflect on your accomplishments and progress. Write them down in a journal or notebook. This can help you see how far you have come and remind you of the progress you have made.

10.7 Share your successes:

Share your successes with others. Tell your family and friends about your accomplishments. This can help you feel proud of yourself and also provide you with encouragement and support from others.

10.8 Treat yourself:

Treat yourself to something special when you reach a milestone or achieve a goal. This could be something as simple as going out for a nice meal or treating yourself to a new book or piece of clothing.

10.9 Set new goals:

Setting new goals can be a great way to celebrate your successes and progress. When you reach a milestone, take some time to think about what you want to achieve next. Setting new goals can help you stay focused and motivated.

10.10 Celebrate with others:

Celebrate your successes and progress with others. Throw a party or get together with friends and family. This can be a great way to share your accomplishments and feel supported by those around you.

In conclusion, celebrating your successes and progress along the way is an essential part of achieving financial success. It helps boost your morale, provides motivation, reinforces positive behavior, and builds resilience. By taking the time to celebrate your accomplishments, you can stay focused on your long-term goals and stay motivated to achieve them.

Part 4 Complete

Part 5

The Power of Visualization

Visualization is a powerful tool for creating the life we want. In this chapter, you will learn how to use visualization to manifest their financial goals and dreams. I will provide practical exercises and techniques for harnessing the power of visualization.

Chapter 1

1.1 The Importance of Surrounding Yourself with Positive Influences

Surrounding yourself with positive influences can have a significant impact on your life and overall well-being. The people you spend time with, the media you consume, and the environments you frequent can all shape your thoughts, beliefs, and attitudes. When you surround yourself with positive influences, you can experience a multitude of benefits, including improved mental health, increased self-esteem, greater motivation, and more success in achieving your goals. In this article, we will explore the importance of surrounding yourself with positive influences in more detail.

1.2 Positive influences can improve your mental health:

The people you surround yourself with can have a significant impact on your mental health. When you spend time with positive, supportive people, you are more likely to feel happier, more confident, and less stressed. Positive people can offer encouragement, advice, and a listening ear when you need it most. They can also help you to see the world in a more positive light and challenge negative thoughts and beliefs.

On the other hand, spending time with negative or toxic people can have the opposite effect. Negative people can drain your energy, lower your mood, and make you feel anxious or unhappy. They can also reinforce negative thoughts and beliefs and make it harder for you to see the good in the world. Therefore, it is important to surround yourself with positive influences to improve your mental health and overall well-being.

1.3 Positive influences can increase your self-esteem:

Your self-esteem refers to your overall sense of self-worth and confidence. When you surround yourself with positive influences, you are more likely to feel good about yourself and your abilities. Positive people can offer praise, encouragement, and recognition for your accomplishments, which can help to boost your self-esteem. They can also offer constructive feedback and support to help you improve in areas where you may be struggling.

In contrast, spending time with negative or critical people can lower your self-esteem and make you doubt your abilities. Negative people may criticize, belittle, or undermine you, which can make you feel unworthy or incompetent. Therefore, it is important to surround yourself with positive influences to increase your self-esteem and confidence.

1.4 Positive influences can motivate and inspire you:

Positive influences can also motivate and inspire you to achieve your goals and reach your full potential. When you spend time with people who are passionate, ambitious, and driven, you are more likely to adopt these qualities yourself. Positive people can offer advice, guidance, and support to help you achieve your goals, and can also provide a sense of accountability to help you stay on track.

In contrast, spending time with people who lack motivation or ambition can make it harder for you to achieve your goals. Negative people may discourage or criticize your efforts, which can lead to feelings of self-doubt or frustration. Therefore, it is important to surround yourself with positive influences to stay motivated and inspired.

1.5 Positive influences can lead to greater success:

Surrounding yourself with positive influences can also lead to greater success in achieving your goals. Positive people can offer support, advice, and networking opportunities to help you advance in your career or achieve your personal goals. They can also provide a sense of community and connection, which can help you to feel more confident and empowered.

In contrast, spending time with negative or unsupportive people can hinder your success. Negative people may discourage or undermine your efforts, which can make it harder for you to achieve your goals. Therefore, it is important to surround yourself with positive influences to increase your chances of success.

1.6 Tips for surrounding yourself with positive influences:

Identify positive role models: Look for people who inspire you and have achieved the kind of success you aspire to in your personal or professional life. These could be people in your family, friends, coworkers, or even public figures. Follow their journey and learn from their experiences.

1.7 Build a support network:

Surround yourself with people who will uplift you, provide encouragement, and offer a listening ear when you need it. This could be friends, family, colleagues, or even a professional support group. It's important to have people who will be there for you through the ups and downs of life.

1.8 Limit exposure to negativity:

Avoid people or situations that bring you down or create negativity in your life. This could include limiting your time on social media, avoiding gossip or negative talk, and setting boundaries with people who drain your energy.

1.9 Join positive communities:

Joining a community of like-minded individuals who share your goals and values can be a great way to surround yourself with positive influences. This could be a group focused on personal development, a hobby or interest group, or even an online community.

1.10 Engage in positive self-talk:

Your own inner dialogue can be a powerful influence on your mindset and overall well-being. Practice positive self-talk and focus on your strengths and accomplishments, rather than dwelling on negative thoughts or self-doubt.

1.11 Seek out mentors:

Mentors can provide guidance and support as you work towards your goals. Look for people who have achieved success in your field or area of interest and reach out to them for advice and guidance.

1.12 Read positive books and articles:

Surround yourself with positive influences by reading books, articles, and other materials that inspire and uplift you. Look for resources that offer practical advice and strategies for achieving success and overcoming challenges.

In conclusion, surrounding yourself with positive influences is essential for achieving your goals and maintaining a positive mindset. By identifying positive role models, building a support network, limiting exposure to negativity, joining positive communities, engaging in positive self-talk, seeking out mentors, and reading positive materials, you can create a positive environment that supports your growth and success.

Chapter 2

2.1 Identifying Negative Influences and Detrimental Habits

Identifying negative influences and detrimental habits is crucial to achieving a positive and fulfilling life. Negative influences can come from people, situations, or even our own habits and thought patterns. These influences can hinder our progress, drain our energy, and prevent us from reaching our goals. Therefore, it is important to identify these negative influences and take steps to eliminate them from our lives.

Here are some tips for identifying negative influences and detrimental habits:

2.2 Reflect on your thoughts and emotions:

Our thoughts and emotions are strong indicators of the negative influences in our lives. If you feel anxious, stressed, or overwhelmed, take a moment to reflect on the source of those feelings. Are there people or situations in your life that are causing these negative emotions? If so, it may be time to reevaluate those relationships or situations.

2.3 Pay attention to your behavior:

Our behavior is often a reflection of our habits and thought patterns. If you find yourself engaging in negative behaviors, such as procrastination or self-sabotage, take a step back and reflect on the root cause of those behaviors. Are there habits or thought patterns that are contributing to these behaviors? Once you identify the source of these negative behaviors, you can take steps to change them.

2.4 Evaluate your relationships:

The people we surround ourselves with have a significant impact on our lives. Evaluate your relationships and consider the impact they are having on your well-being. Are there people in your life who are constantly negative or critical? Are there people who drain your energy or make you feel bad about yourself? It may be time to distance yourself from these individuals or seek out more positive relationships.

2.5 Examine your habits:

Our habits are powerful influencers on our daily lives. Examine your habits and consider whether they are contributing to a negative mindset or lifestyle. For example, if you spend a lot of time on social media or watching TV, consider whether these habits are contributing to a negative mindset or taking away from more positive activities, such as exercise or spending time with loved ones.

2.6 Identify your triggers:

We all have triggers that can lead to negative thoughts or emotions. Identify your triggers and take steps to avoid them or mitigate their impact. For example, if you know that watching the news or engaging in political debates on social media triggers negative emotions, consider limiting your exposure to these activities.

2.7 Seek out positive influences:

Surrounding yourself with positive influences can help counteract the negative influences in your life. Seek out positive relationships, activities, and environments that contribute to a positive mindset and lifestyle. This could include spending time with supportive friends and family members, engaging in hobbies that bring you joy, or spending time in nature.

2.8 Practice self-care:

Taking care of yourself is an important part of identifying and eliminating negative influences from your life. Practice self-care activities, such as exercise, meditation, or journaling, to help you manage stress and maintain a positive mindset.

2.9 Keep a journal:

Write down your thoughts, feelings, and actions throughout the day. This can help you identify patterns in your behavior and identify situations or people that trigger negative thoughts or emotions.

Evaluate your relationships:

Take a closer look at the people in your life and how they make you feel. Are there people who bring you down or make you feel bad about yourself? Are there people who constantly criticize or judge you? These are negative influences that you may need to distance yourself from.

2.10 Assess your habits:

Think about your daily routines and habits. Are there habits that are detrimental to your health, such as smoking or drinking too much alcohol? Are there habits that are negatively impacting your mental or emotional well-being, such as staying up too late or spending too much time on social media?

2.11 Identify triggers:

Think about the situations or people that trigger negative thoughts or emotions. Once you have identified your triggers, you can develop strategies to avoid or manage them.

2.12 Seek feedback:

Ask for feedback from people you trust and respect. They may be able to provide insight into negative behaviors or habits that you may not be aware of.

2.13 Pay attention to your feelings:

Pay attention to how you feel after spending time with certain people or engaging in certain activities. If you feel drained, stressed, or unhappy, these may be signs of negative influences or detrimental habits.

In conclusion, surrounding yourself with positive influences is essential for achieving your goals and maintaining a positive mindset. By identifying positive role models, building a support network, limiting exposure to negativity, joining positive communities, engaging in positive self-talk, seeking out mentors, and reading positive materials, you can create a positive environment that supports your growth and success.

Chapter 3

3.1 Strategies for Eliminating Negative Influences from Your Life

We all have people or habits in our lives that bring us down, drain our energy, or hinder our personal growth. These negative influences can affect us in many ways, including our mental and emotional well-being, our relationships, and even our career or financial success. Therefore, it is essential to identify and eliminate these negative influences to create a healthier and more fulfilling life. Here are some strategies for doing so:

3.2 Identify the negative influences:

The first step is to become aware of the negative influences in your life. This can include people who are constantly negative, critical, or unsupportive, as well as habits that are harmful to your well-being, such as excessive drinking or drug use, overeating, or procrastination. Take some time to reflect on the people and habits that are holding you back and write them down.

3.3 Set boundaries:

Once you have identified the negative influences in your life, it is important to set boundaries to protect yourself from them. This may mean limiting your contact with certain people or avoiding situations where you are likely to engage in harmful habits. Be clear and assertive about your boundaries, and communicate them clearly to others.

3.4 Surround yourself with positive influences:

To counteract the negative influences in your life, surround yourself with positive influences that support your goals and aspirations. This can include spending time with people who are positive, supportive, and encouraging, and engaging in activities that make you feel good and contribute to your well-being.

3.5 Practice self-care:

Taking care of yourself is essential for eliminating negative influences from your life. Make time for activities that bring you joy and relaxation, such as exercise, meditation, or reading. Eat a healthy, balanced diet, get enough sleep, and prioritize your mental and emotional well-being.

3.6 Seek professional help:

If you are struggling to eliminate negative influences from your life or are dealing with more serious issues such as addiction or mental health problems, seek professional help. A therapist or counselor can provide you with the support, guidance, and tools you need to overcome these challenges and create a healthier, happier life.

3.7 Set boundaries:

It's important to set clear boundaries with people who have a negative influence on your life. This means saying "no" to invitations or requests that don't align with your values and goals. It also means limiting your exposure to people who bring you down or make you feel bad about yourself.

3.8 Practice self-care:

Taking care of yourself physically, emotionally, and mentally is crucial to eliminating negative influences from your life. This means getting enough sleep, eating a healthy diet, exercising regularly, and engaging in activities that bring you joy and fulfillment.

3.9 Seek support:

Surround yourself with positive and supportive people who encourage you to be your best self. Joining a support group, seeking therapy, or working with a life coach can also provide valuable guidance and support.

3.10 Focus on your goals:

Keep your focus on your goals and what you want to achieve in life. When you have a clear vision of what you want, it becomes easier to eliminate negative influences that don't align with your vision.

3.11 Learn to say "no":

Saying "no" can be difficult, especially if you're used to people-pleasing or accommodating others at the expense of your own well-being. However, learning to say "no" is an important part of eliminating negative influences from your life.

3.12 Let go of toxic relationships:

Sometimes, despite your best efforts, it may be necessary to let go of toxic relationships. This may mean ending a friendship, romantic relationship, or even a family relationship that is negatively impacting your life. While it can be difficult, it's important to prioritize your own well-being and surround yourself with positive influences.

3.13 Focus on your goals:

Finally, stay focused on your goals and aspirations, and keep reminding yourself why you want to eliminate these negative influences from your life. Whether it is to improve your mental and emotional well-being, enhance your relationships, or achieve greater success in your career or personal life, staying focused on your goals can help you stay motivated and on track.

Another strategy is to actively seek out positive influences and role models. This may involve joining a community or group with similar interests and values, attending events and conferences related to your passions, or seeking out mentors who can offer guidance and support.

Eliminating negative influences from your life is not always easy, but it is essential for creating a healthier and more fulfilling life. By setting boundaries, surrounding yourself with positive influences, practicing self-care, seeking professional help, and staying focused on your goals, you can take control of your life and create the happiness and success you deserve.

Overall, identifying and eliminating negative influences from our lives can be a challenging but necessary process in creating a positive and fulfilling life. It requires a willingness to reflect on our values, boundaries, and priorities, as well as the courage to make difficult decisions and take action to create a healthier and more supportive environment for ourselves.

Chapter 4

4.1 How to Cultivate Positive Relationships and Connections

Building positive relationships and connections with others is an important aspect of a fulfilling and happy life. Positive relationships provide support, encouragement, and inspiration, and they can help you grow and develop as a person. When it comes to financial success, having positive relationships can also play a key role. People who have strong, positive relationships tend to have better financial outcomes, whether it's through shared financial goals or emotional support during tough financial times.

In this article, we will explore some strategies for cultivating positive relationships and connections in your life.

4.2 Focus on building mutual trust and respect:

One of the most important elements of a positive relationship is mutual trust and respect. Without trust and respect, it can be difficult to build a lasting and positive connection with someone. To cultivate trust and respect, be honest and transparent with your communication, and listen actively to the other person. Respect their opinions and beliefs, even if they differ from your own. Show empathy and kindness, and be willing to compromise and work through disagreements in a respectful and constructive manner.

4.3 Be authentic and true to yourself:

When building positive relationships, it's important to be authentic and true to yourself. Pretending to be someone you're not or hiding your true thoughts and feelings can create barriers and prevent authentic connections from forming. Embrace your strengths and weaknesses, and be honest about your goals and aspirations. This will help attract like-minded individuals who share your values and beliefs, and who can provide genuine support and encouragement.

4.4 Engage in active listening and effective communication:

Effective communication is essential to building positive relationships. Engage in active listening by paying close attention to what the other person is saying, and avoid interrupting or talking over them. Use open-ended questions to encourage dialogue and invite the other person to share their thoughts and feelings. Be aware of your tone and body language, as they can communicate just as much as your words.

4.5 Foster a sense of community and shared interests:

Shared interests and experiences can help foster a sense of community and belonging, which can be an important foundation for positive relationships. Participate in group activities or join clubs or organizations that align with your interests and passions. This can help you connect with like-minded individuals who share your values and beliefs, and who can provide emotional support and encouragement.

4.6 Practice kindness and generosity:

Small acts of kindness and generosity can go a long way in building positive relationships. Take the time to express gratitude and appreciation for the people in your life, and be willing to lend a helping hand when they need it. Volunteer your time or resources for causes that are important to you, and encourage others to do the same. These actions can help strengthen your connections with others and create a positive and supportive network.

4.7 Embrace diversity and different perspectives:

Positive relationships can also be formed by embracing diversity and different perspectives. Be open to learning about different cultures, backgrounds, and experiences, and seek to understand and appreciate the differences. This can help broaden your own perspective and provide opportunities for personal growth and development.

4.8 Set boundaries and prioritize your well-being:

While cultivating positive relationships is important, it's also important to set boundaries and prioritize your well-being. Be mindful of your own needs and limitations, and communicate them clearly to the people in your life. Respect others' boundaries as well, and avoid overextending yourself or sacrificing your own well-being for the sake of a relationship.

4.9 Be present:

When spending time with others, make an effort to be fully present and engaged in the conversation. Avoid distractions like phones or other devices that can take away from the interaction.

4.10 Listen actively:

Listening is a key component of effective communication and building positive relationships. Show that you are truly interested in what the other person has to say by actively listening and asking thoughtful questions.

4.11 Show appreciation:

A simple "thank you" or expression of gratitude can go a long way in building positive relationships. Take the time to acknowledge and show appreciation for the people in your life who make a positive impact.

4.12 Practice empathy:

Empathy involves putting yourself in someone else's shoes and understanding their perspective. By practicing empathy, you can deepen your connections with others and build more positive relationships.

4.13 Practice forgiveness:

No one is perfect, and conflicts and misunderstandings are bound to happen in any relationship. Practice forgiveness by letting go of grudges and resentments, and work towards resolving conflicts in a constructive and positive way.

4.14 Be supportive:

Be there for the people in your life when they need support or encouragement. This could mean offering a listening ear, providing practical assistance, or simply being a source of positivity and motivation.

4.15 Build trust:

Trust is a crucial component of any healthy relationship. To build trust, be honest and transparent in your communication, follow through on your commitments, and demonstrate your reliability and dependability.

4.16 Seek out like-minded individuals:

Surround yourself with people who share your values and interests. This can help you build deeper connections and create a sense of community.

4.17 Practice inclusivity:

Make an effort to include people from diverse backgrounds and perspectives in your social circles. This can help you broaden your perspectives, learn from others, and build more meaningful relationships.

4.18 Make time for social activities:

Whether it's joining a club or group, attending social events, or simply spending time with friends and family, make time for social activities that allow you to connect with others and build positive relationships.

In conclusion, cultivating positive relationships and connections is essential for a fulfilling and happy life. By focusing on mutual trust and respect, authenticity, effective communication, shared interests, kindness and generosity, diversity and different perspectives, and setting boundaries and prioritizing your well-being, you can build a positive and supportive network of people who will help you grow and succeed.

Chapter 5

5.1 Building a Support System of Like-Minded Individuals

Building a support system of like-minded individuals can be a powerful way to cultivate positive relationships and connections. When you surround yourself with people who share similar goals, values, and interests, you can feel more motivated, inspired, and supported in your own pursuits. Here are some strategies for building a support system of like-minded individuals:

Join groups or communities related to your interests or goals: Whether it's a professional organization, a hobby group, or a social club, there are likely groups or communities that share your interests and goals. Joining these groups can provide you with opportunities to meet and connect with like-minded individuals who can offer support, advice, and encouragement.

5.2 Be present:

When spending time with others, make an effort to be fully present and engaged in the conversation. Avoid distractions like phones or other devices that can take away from the interaction.

5.3 Listen actively:

Listening is a key component of effective communication and building positive relationships. Show that you are truly interested in what the other person has to say by actively listening and asking thoughtful questions.

5.4 Show appreciation:

A simple "thank you" or expression of gratitude can go a long way in building positive relationships. Take the time to acknowledge and show appreciation for the people in your life who make a positive impact.

5.5 Practice empathy:

Empathy involves putting yourself in someone else's shoes and understanding their perspective. By practicing empathy, you can deepen your connections with others and build more positive relationships.

5.6 Practice forgiveness:

No one is perfect, and conflicts and misunderstandings are bound to happen in any relationship. Practice forgiveness by letting go of grudges and resentments, and work towards resolving conflicts in a constructive and positive way.

5.7 Be supportive:

Be there for the people in your life when they need support or encouragement. This could mean offering a listening ear, providing practical assistance, or simply being a source of positivity and motivation.

5.8 Build trust:

Trust is a crucial component of any healthy relationship. To build trust, be honest and transparent in your communication, follow through on your commitments, and demonstrate your reliability and dependability.

5.9 Seek out like-minded individuals:

Surround yourself with people who share your values and interests. This can help you build deeper connections and create a sense of community.

5.10 Practice inclusivity:

Make an effort to include people from diverse backgrounds and perspectives in your social circles. This can help you broaden your perspectives, learn from others, and build more meaningful relationships.

5.11 Make time for social activities:

Whether it's joining a club or group, attending social events, or simply spending time with friends and family, make time for social activities that allow you to connect with others and build positive relationships.

5.12 Attend networking events:

Networking events can be a great way to meet new people and expand your professional and social circles. Look for events related to your industry or interests, and be prepared to introduce yourself and make meaningful connections.

5.13 Utilize social media:

Social media can be a powerful tool for connecting with like-minded individuals. Joining online communities or groups related to your interests or goals can provide you with opportunities to connect with people all over the world who share your passions.

5.14 Volunteer or get involved in community service:

Volunteering or getting involved in community service can be a great way to meet people who share your values and interests. Not only can you make a positive impact in your community, but you can also build meaningful connections with other volunteers and community members.

5.15 Take classes or attend workshops:

Taking classes or attending workshops related to your interests or goals can provide you with opportunities to meet and connect with like-minded individuals. Whether it's a cooking class, a yoga workshop, or a business seminar, you can learn new skills and make valuable connections in the process.

5.16 Be open and approachable:

Building positive relationships and connections requires being open and approachable. Smile, make eye contact, and be willing to engage in conversation with others. By being friendly and approachable, you can attract like-minded individuals who are interested in building positive relationships.

5.17 Be authentic and genuine:

Authenticity and genuineness are important traits when building positive relationships and connections. Be true to yourself and your values, and be honest and transparent in your interactions with others. By being authentic and genuine, you can attract like-minded individuals who share your values and appreciate your authenticity.

Overall, building a support system of like-minded individuals requires effort, patience, and a willingness to put yourself out there. By taking proactive steps to connect with others who share your goals and interests, you can build a network of positive relationships that can support and inspire you on your journey.

Chapter 6

6.1 The Power of Learning from Successful Mentors and Role Models

Learning from successful mentors and role models can be a powerful tool in achieving personal and professional growth. Mentors and role models can offer guidance, advice, and insights based on their own experiences and expertise, which can help individuals learn valuable lessons and avoid pitfalls. By studying the successes and strategies of those who have achieved success in areas that are important to us, we can gain a better understanding of what it takes to achieve our own goals and objectives.

Here are some ways to leverage the power of learning from successful mentors and role models:

6.2 Identify individuals who have achieved success in areas that are important to you:

Think about the specific goals and objectives that you want to achieve, and then identify individuals who have already achieved success in those areas. This might include successful entrepreneurs, business leaders, athletes, artists, or other professionals.

6.3 Study their successes and strategies:

Once you have identified your mentors and role models, study their successes and strategies. This might involve reading their books or articles, watching their interviews or speeches, attending their seminars or workshops, or connecting with them directly through social media or email.

6.4 Learn from their mistakes and failures:

While it's important to study the successes of your mentors and role models, it's equally important to learn from their mistakes and failures. By understanding the challenges and obstacles they faced along the way, you can gain valuable insights into how to avoid similar pitfalls.

6.5 Seek their guidance and advice:

If possible, seek out your mentors and role models for guidance and advice. This might involve connecting with them directly through email or social media, attending their workshops or seminars, or even scheduling a one-on-one consultation or mentoring session.

6.6 Model their behavior and habits:

Finally, model the behavior and habits of your mentors and role models. This might involve adopting their mindset, daily habits, or approach to work and life. By modeling the behavior of successful individuals, you can begin to develop the same qualities and characteristics that have contributed to their success.

6.7 Access to Experience and Expertise:

A mentor or role model who has achieved success in your field of interest can provide valuable insights and advice based on their experience and expertise. By learning from their successes and failures, you can gain a deeper understanding of what it takes to succeed and avoid making the same mistakes.

6.8 Networking Opportunities:

Successful mentors and role models can also introduce you to others in your field who can offer additional insights and connections. This can help you build your own network of contacts, which can be invaluable when it comes to finding new opportunities and advancing your career.

6.9 Personal Growth:

A successful mentor or role model can also provide guidance and support when it comes to personal growth and development. They can offer insights into how to overcome challenges and develop the skills and qualities needed to achieve success.

6.10 Inspiration and Motivation:

Seeing someone who has achieved success in your field can be incredibly motivating and inspiring. A successful mentor or role model can serve as a powerful reminder that it is possible to achieve your goals, even in the face of obstacles.

6.11 Accountability:

A mentor or role model can also help hold you accountable to your goals and commitments. By checking in with you regularly and offering feedback and advice, they can help you stay on track and overcome any obstacles that may arise.

The Wealth mindset

By learning from successful mentors and role models, you can gain valuable insights and guidance that can help you achieve your own personal and professional goals. Whether you're an entrepreneur, athlete, artist, or other professional, there are always individuals who have achieved success in areas that are important to you. By studying their successes and strategies, learning from their mistakes and failures, seeking their guidance and advice, and modeling their behavior and habits, you can develop the skills and qualities necessary to achieve your own success.

Overall, learning from successful mentors and role models can be a powerful tool in achieving your own success. By seeking out and building relationships with those who have achieved what you aspire to, you can gain valuable insights, build your network, and stay motivated and inspired as you pursue your own goals.

Chapter 7

7.1 Techniques for Developing Stronger Emotional Intelligence

Emotional intelligence refers to the ability to identify and manage one's own emotions as well as the emotions of others. Developing stronger emotional intelligence can have numerous benefits, including improved communication skills, better decision-making abilities, and greater self-awareness. Here are some techniques that can help in developing stronger emotional intelligence:

7.2 Practice self-awareness:

One of the key components of emotional intelligence is self-awareness. This involves being able to recognize your own emotions and understand how they impact your thoughts and behaviors. To develop self-awareness, it can be helpful to regularly reflect on your emotions and the reasons behind them.

7.3 Develop empathy:

Empathy is the ability to understand and relate to the emotions of others. To develop empathy, it is important to actively listen to others and try to put yourself in their shoes. This can help to build stronger relationships and improve communication skills.

7.4 Practice mindfulness:

Mindfulness involves being present in the moment and observing your thoughts and emotions without judgment. Regular mindfulness practice can help to improve emotional regulation and reduce stress and anxiety.

7.5 Improve communication skills:

Effective communication is key to developing strong relationships and managing emotions. To improve communication skills, it can be helpful to practice active listening, be aware of nonverbal cues, and use "I" statements instead of "you'r" statements.

7.6 Practice emotional regulation:

Emotional regulation involves being able to manage your own emotions and respond appropriately to the emotions of others. Techniques for improving emotional regulation can include deep breathing exercises, practicing gratitude, and cognitive reappraisal.

7.7 Seek feedback:

Seeking feedback from others can be a helpful way to gain insight into your own emotional intelligence and identify areas for improvement.

7.8 Cultivate positive relationships:

Building positive relationships with others can help to improve emotional intelligence by providing opportunities for social support and connection.

7.9 Practice self-awareness:

The first step to developing emotional intelligence is to become more self-aware. This involves identifying your own emotions and understanding how they influence your thoughts and behaviors. Start by taking time to reflect on your feelings and reactions in different situations. You can also try keeping a journal or talking to a trusted friend or therapist to help you gain deeper insights into your emotions.

7.10 Learn to manage your emotions:

Once you have developed a greater sense of self-awareness, you can start to work on managing your emotions more effectively. This involves learning techniques for regulating your emotions and staying calm in challenging situations. Some helpful strategies include deep breathing, meditation, exercise, and practicing mindfulness.

7.11 Develop empathy:

Another key aspect of emotional intelligence is empathy, or the ability to understand and connect with the emotions of others. To develop this skill, try to put yourself in other people's shoes and consider how they might be feeling in different situations. You can also practice active listening, which involves giving your full attention to someone and responding thoughtfully to what they are saying.

7.12 Build strong relationships:

Building strong relationships with others is an important part of developing emotional intelligence. This involves cultivating open and honest communication, showing empathy and compassion, and working to resolve conflicts in a constructive way. You can also work on developing your social skills by practicing effective communication, being open to feedback, and learning to adapt your communication style to different people and situations.

7.13 Practice self-care:

Finally, it's important to take care of yourself in order to develop emotional intelligence. This means making time for activities that you enjoy, taking care of your physical health, and seeking support when you need it. When you are feeling stressed or overwhelmed, it can be difficult to manage your emotions effectively, so taking steps to reduce stress and prioritize your own well-being can help you develop stronger emotional intelligence over time.

Overall, developing stronger emotional intelligence requires consistent practice and self-reflection. By incorporating these techniques into your daily life, you can improve your ability to manage emotions, build stronger relationships, and achieve greater success in both personal and professional settings.

Chapter 8

8.1 Overcoming Fear and Anxiety in Networking and Social Situations

Networking and social situations can be intimidating for many people, especially if they struggle with fear and anxiety. However, building strong connections and relationships is crucial for personal and professional growth. Overcoming these fears and anxieties can open up new opportunities and lead to personal and professional success. In this article, we will explore techniques for overcoming fear and anxiety in networking and social situations.

8.2 Recognize your fear and anxiety:

The first step in overcoming fear and anxiety is to recognize and acknowledge it. It is important to understand that fear and anxiety are normal emotions and that many people experience them in social situations. Once you recognize and accept your fear and anxiety, you can take steps to address it.

8.3 Practice deep breathing and relaxation techniques:

Deep breathing and relaxation techniques can help calm your nerves and reduce anxiety. Before entering a networking event or social situation, take a few minutes to practice deep breathing or relaxation techniques. This can help you feel more relaxed and focused.

8.4 Set realistic goals and expectations:

Setting realistic goals and expectations can help you feel more comfortable and confident in social situations. For example, if you are attending a networking event, set a goal to introduce yourself to two or three people. This can help you focus on a specific task and feel more in control of the situation.

8.5 Prepare for the event:

Preparation is key to reducing anxiety in social situations. Take some time to research the event and the people who will be attending. This can help you feel more prepared and confident. Practice introducing yourself and have a few conversation starters ready.

8.6 Shift your focus:

Instead of focusing on your fear and anxiety, try shifting your focus to the people you are talking to. Ask questions and listen attentively. This can help you feel more engaged and present in the conversation.

8.7 Use positive self-talk:

Negative self-talk can increase anxiety and make social situations more challenging. Practice using positive self-talk to boost your confidence and reduce anxiety. For example, tell yourself that you are capable and confident.

8.8 Gradual exposure:

Gradual exposure is a technique that involves gradually exposing yourself to situations that make you anxious. This can help you build up your tolerance and reduce anxiety over time. Start by attending smaller social events or networking with people you are already familiar with. As you become more comfortable, gradually increase the size and scope of your social engagements.

8.9 Seek support:

Seeking support from friends, family, or a therapist can be helpful in overcoming fear and anxiety in social situations. They can provide encouragement, advice, and support as you navigate challenging social situations.

8.10 Visualize success:

Before attending a social event or networking opportunity, take some time to visualize yourself succeeding. Imagine yourself confidently approaching people, engaging in conversations, and making meaningful connections. Visualize yourself feeling calm, relaxed, and in control.

8.11 Challenge negative self-talk:

Negative self-talk can be a major contributor to fear and anxiety. If you find yourself thinking things like "I'm not good enough" or "No one will like me," challenge those thoughts with evidence to the contrary. For example, if you're worried that you're not interesting enough to talk to, remind yourself of some interesting things about yourself or some recent successes you've had.

8.12 Practice mindfulness:

Mindfulness techniques, such as deep breathing or meditation, can be helpful in reducing anxiety and helping you stay present in the moment. If you're feeling anxious in a social situation, try taking a few deep breaths and focusing on the present moment rather than worrying about what might happen in the future.

8.13 Be kind to yourself:

Remember that everyone experiences fear and anxiety in social situations from time to time, and it's okay to feel nervous. Treat yourself with kindness and compassion, and don't beat yourself up if things don't go exactly as planned.

8.14 Seek support:

If fear and anxiety are significantly impacting your ability to network and connect with others, don't be afraid to seek support. Consider talking to a therapist or coach who can help you develop coping strategies and overcome your fears. You might also consider joining a support group for people who struggle with social anxiety or attending networking events with a friend who can provide emotional support.

In conclusion, fear and anxiety in networking and social situations are common, but they do not have to hold you back. By recognizing your fear and anxiety, practicing relaxation techniques, setting realistic goals, preparing for the event, shifting your focus, using positive self-talk, gradual exposure, and seeking support, you can overcome these challenges and build strong relationships and connections.

Chapter 9

9.1 How to Communicate Effectively and Persuasively

Effective communication is an essential life skill that can greatly impact our personal and professional relationships. Whether you are trying to persuade someone to agree with your point of view or simply convey information, it's crucial to know how to communicate in a way that is clear, concise, and persuasive. In this article, we will discuss techniques for effective communication and persuasion.

9.2 Know your audience:

Before you begin communicating, it's essential to know who you're communicating with. This knowledge can help you tailor your message to the audience and use language and tone that will resonate with them.

9.3 Plan your message:

Before you start communicating, take some time to plan your message. This process can help you clarify your thoughts and organize your message in a logical and persuasive manner.

9.4 Be clear and concise:

Effective communication is about clarity and concision. Use simple language and avoid jargon or technical terms that may confuse your audience. Make your message easy to understand and concise.

9.5 Listen actively:

Communication is a two-way street. It's important to listen actively to the other person and understand their perspective. Active listening involves paying attention to the other person's words, tone, and body language.

9.6 Use body language:

Body language can be a powerful tool for effective communication. Using gestures, facial expressions, and posture can help emphasize your message and convey emotion.

9.7 Avoid distractions:

When communicating, it's important to avoid distractions that can interfere with your message. Find a quiet place to talk and minimize interruptions.

9.8 Use stories and anecdotes:

Stories and anecdotes can be a powerful way to communicate a message. They can help make your message more memorable and engaging.

9.9 Use persuasive language:

Persuasive language can help you convince your audience to agree with your message. Use language that is positive, active, and confident.

9.10 Use repetition:

Repetition can help reinforce your message and make it more memorable. Use key phrases or ideas multiple times throughout your message.

9.11 Be respectful:

Respectful communication is key to building positive relationships. Treat the other person with kindness and respect, even if you disagree with their perspective.

Effective communication is a crucial skill that can help individuals in various aspects of life, from personal relationships to professional success. It involves transmitting ideas, thoughts, or information clearly and accurately to another person or group of people. Communication can take many forms, including verbal, nonverbal, written, and visual.

To communicate effectively, individuals need to understand the importance of using the right tone, language, and body language. They also need to consider their audience and adjust their communication style accordingly. Here are some techniques for developing effective communication skills:

9.12 Nonverbal communication:

Nonverbal communication includes body language, facial expressions, and tone of voice. It is an essential aspect of effective communication, as it can convey more than words alone. Individuals should be aware of their nonverbal cues and make sure they align with their message.

9.13 Empathy:

Empathy involves understanding and sharing the feelings of another person. It is a vital component of effective communication, as it can help build trust and rapport. Individuals can show empathy by acknowledging the other person's emotions and responding in a supportive manner.

9.14 Clarity and conciseness:

Clear and concise communication is essential in ensuring that the message is understood correctly. Individuals should avoid using jargon, complex terms, or vague language. Instead, they should use simple, straightforward language and be precise in their message.

9.15 Assertiveness:

Assertiveness involves expressing opinions, thoughts, and feelings in a confident and respectful manner. It is a crucial aspect of effective communication, as it can help individuals stand up for themselves while maintaining positive relationships. Individuals can practice assertiveness by using "I" statements, being direct and specific, and focusing on the issue rather than the person.

9.16 Flexibility:

Effective communication requires being flexible and adapting to different communication styles and situations. Individuals should be willing to adjust their communication style depending on the audience, context, and message they want to convey.

9.17 Feedback:

Feedback is an essential aspect of effective communication, as it can help individuals improve their communication skills. Individuals should be open to receiving feedback, both positive and negative, and use it to improve their communication skills.

9.18 Practice:

Like any skill, effective communication requires practice. Individuals can practice by engaging in conversations, asking for feedback, and reflecting on their communication style.

In conclusion, effective communication skills are essential for success in various aspects of life. By practicing active listening, using nonverbal communication, showing empathy, being clear and concise, practicing assertiveness, being flexible, seeking feedback, and practicing regularly, individuals can improve their communication skills and build stronger relationships.

Chapter 10

10.1 Cultivating a Mindset of Abundance and Generosity

Cultivating a mindset of abundance and generosity can have a profound impact on one's life, relationships, and overall sense of well-being. When we approach life with a mindset of abundance, we believe that there is enough to go around and that we have the resources we need to achieve our goals. This perspective can be a powerful antidote to feelings of scarcity and fear, which can limit our ability to take risks and pursue our dreams.

At the same time, cultivating a mindset of generosity means approaching others with an open heart and a willingness to give of ourselves. This can take many forms, from offering a kind word or gesture to volunteering our time or resources to support those in need. By adopting a generous spirit, we can build deeper connections with others and contribute to a more positive and supportive community.

Here are some strategies for cultivating a mindset of abundance and generosity:

10.2 Practice gratitude:

One of the simplest ways to cultivate a mindset of abundance is to focus on what we already have and express gratitude for it. This could involve taking time each day to reflect on the things we are grateful for, such as our health, our relationships, or our accomplishments.

By cultivating a sense of abundance around what we already have, we can create a foundation of positivity and abundance to build upon.

10.3 Focus on possibilities:

When we approach life with a mindset of abundance, we are more likely to see opportunities and possibilities rather than obstacles and limitations. Instead of focusing on what we don't have or what we can't do, we can shift our attention to what we do have and what we can do. This can help us to stay motivated and hopeful, even in the face of challenges.

10.4 Give generously:

Giving generously doesn't necessarily mean giving away all our time or resources, but it does mean approaching others with an open heart and a willingness to share. This could involve offering a listening ear to a friend in need, volunteering at a local charity, or simply offering a kind word or gesture to someone who is struggling. By giving generously, we can contribute to a more positive and supportive community and build deeper connections with others.

10.5 Seek out positive influences:

Surrounding ourselves with positive influences can help to reinforce a mindset of abundance and generosity. This could involve seeking out mentors or role models who embody these qualities, or simply spending time with friends and family members who share our values. By surrounding ourselves with positive influences, we can build a supportive network of people who inspire us to be our best selves.

10.6 Challenge scarcity thinking:

Scarcity thinking is the belief that there is not enough to go around and that we must compete with others to get what we need. This mindset can be limiting and self-defeating, as it can lead to feelings of fear, anxiety, and inadequacy. By challenging scarcity thinking and embracing a mindset of abundance, we can break free from these limiting beliefs and approach life with a greater sense of optimism and possibility.

10.7 Practice mindfulness:

Mindfulness involves being present and aware in the moment, without judgment or distraction. By practicing mindfulness, we can cultivate a deeper sense of connection to ourselves and others, and become more attuned to the abundance that surrounds us. This could involve taking time each day to meditate or simply to reflect on our thoughts and feelings.

10.8 Embrace growth and learning:

Finally, cultivating a mindset of abundance and generosity requires a willingness to grow and learn. This could involve seeking out new experiences, taking on new challenges, or simply remaining open to feedback and constructive criticism. By embracing growth and learning, we can continue to expand our horizons and deepen our sense of purpose and fulfillment.

10.9 Giving Back to Others:

Generosity is an important aspect of an abundance mindset. When you give back to others, whether through volunteering, donating to charity, or simply offering a helping hand, you're showing that you have more than enough to share. This not only benefits others but can also bring a sense of fulfillment and purpose to your own life.

10.10 Avoiding Comparison:

Comparing yourself to others is a surefire way to feel like you're lacking in some way. Instead, focus on your own journey and progress. Remember that everyone has their own unique path and that your own successes and achievements are just as valid and important.

10.11 Embracing Change and Growth:

An abundance mindset embraces change and growth rather than fearing it. Instead of being held back by a fear of failure or change, you embrace new opportunities and challenges as they arise. This opens up new possibilities and helps you continue to grow and evolve.

10.12 Surrounding Yourself with Abundance-Minded People:

The people you surround yourself with can greatly influence your mindset. Seek out individuals who have an abundance mindset and are supportive of your goals and aspirations. Their positivity and encouragement can help you cultivate a mindset of abundance and generosity in your own life.

10.13 Finding Joy in the Journey:

Finally, remember that the journey is just as important as the destination. Enjoy the process of pursuing your goals and don't get too caught up in the end result. When you focus on the present moment and find joy in the journey, you're more likely to cultivate a positive, abundance-minded mindset.

In summary, cultivating a mindset of abundance and generosity can have a powerful impact on our lives and relationships. By practicing gratitude, focusing on possibilities, giving generously,

The Wealth mindset

Part 5 Complete

Part 6

The Role of Habits

Habits play a crucial role in shaping our lives. In this chapter, readers will learn how to develop positive habits that support their financial success. I will provide tips for creating a daily routine that aligns with their goals and values.

Chapter 1

1.1 The Importance of Financial Education and Literacy

Financial education and literacy are essential components of achieving long-term financial success and stability. Unfortunately, many individuals lack the knowledge and skills necessary to make informed decisions about their finances, leading to financial struggles and hardship. This is why financial education is so critical, as it empowers individuals with the knowledge and skills they need to make informed decisions about their financial future.

Financial education encompasses a broad range of topics, including budgeting, saving, investing, debt management, retirement planning, and more. It involves learning about personal finance concepts, financial products and services, and how to use them effectively to achieve one's financial goals.

One of the key benefits of financial education is that it can help individuals avoid common financial mistakes and pitfalls. Many people find themselves in debt or struggling financially because they lack basic financial knowledge and skills. By learning about budgeting, saving, and debt management, individuals can develop a better understanding of how to manage their finances and avoid financial hardship.

Financial education can also help individuals plan for the future. This includes setting financial goals, such as saving for a down payment on a home or planning for retirement. With the right knowledge and tools, individuals can make informed decisions about how to achieve these goals and stay on track.

There are many resources available for individuals who want to improve their financial education and literacy. For example, there are financial literacy courses and workshops available online and in-person, as well as books, podcasts, and other resources that provide valuable information about personal finance concepts.

In addition to formal education, there are many other ways to improve one's financial literacy. For example, individuals can start by tracking their expenses and creating a budget to help them manage their money more effectively. They can also seek out the advice of financial professionals, such as financial advisors or accountants, to help them make informed decisions about their finances.

Overall, the importance of financial education and literacy cannot be overstated. With the right knowledge and skills, individuals can make informed decisions about their finances, avoid common financial mistakes, and achieve their long-term financial goals. Financial education and literacy are essential components of achieving long-term financial success and stability. Unfortunately, many individuals lack the knowledge and skills necessary to make informed decisions about their finances, leading to financial struggles and hardship. This is why financial education is so critical, as it empowers individuals with the knowledge and skills they need to make informed decisions about their financial future.

Financial education encompasses a broad range of topics, including budgeting, saving, investing, debt management, retirement planning, and more. It involves learning about personal finance concepts, financial products and services, and how to use them effectively to achieve one's financial goals.

One of the key benefits of financial education is that it can help individuals avoid common financial mistakes and pitfalls. Many people find themselves in debt or struggling financially because they lack basic financial knowledge and skills. By learning about budgeting, saving, and debt management, individuals can develop a better understanding of how to manage their finances and avoid financial hardship.

Financial education can also help individuals plan for the future. This includes setting financial goals, such as saving for a down payment on a home or planning for retirement. With the right knowledge and tools, individuals can make informed decisions about how to achieve these goals and stay on track.

There are many resources available for individuals who want to improve their financial education and literacy. For example, there are financial literacy courses and workshops available online and in-person, as well as books, podcasts, and other resources that provide valuable information about personal finance concepts.

In addition to formal education, there are many other ways to improve one's financial literacy. For example, individuals can start by tracking their expenses and creating a budget to help them manage their money more effectively. They can also seek out the advice of financial professionals, such as financial advisors or accountants, to help them make informed decisions about their finances.

Overall, the importance of financial education and literacy cannot be overstated. With the right knowledge and skills, individuals can make informed decisions about their finances, avoid common financial mistakes, and achieve their long-term financial goals.

Financial education empowers individuals to make informed decisions about their money. Without an understanding of financial concepts such as budgeting, saving, investing, and debt management, individuals are left vulnerable to making poor financial decisions that can have long-lasting consequences.

Financial education is essential for building long-term financial security. Individuals who are financially literate are better equipped to make sound financial decisions throughout their lives, from setting financial goals to creating a retirement plan.

Financial education can help break the cycle of poverty. When individuals have access to financial education, they are better equipped to manage their money and plan for the future. This can help break the cycle of poverty and promote economic mobility.

Financial education can help individuals build wealth. Understanding financial concepts such as compound interest and investment strategies can help individuals build wealth over time, leading to greater financial stability and security.

Financial education is particularly important for marginalized communities. Individuals from low-income communities, women, and people of color are often disproportionately affected by financial instability and lack of access to financial education. Providing financial education can help level the playing field and promote greater economic equality.

Financial education can help individuals avoid financial scams and fraud. Understanding basic financial concepts and knowing how to spot fraudulent schemes can help individuals protect themselves from financial exploitation.

Financial education can help individuals make more informed decisions about their careers. Understanding the financial implications of different career paths, such as the earning potential and job security, can help individuals make more informed decisions about their career choices.

Financial education can help individuals navigate major life events, such as buying a home or starting a family. These events often come with significant financial decisions and obligations, and a lack of financial literacy can lead to costly mistakes.

Financial education is not just for adults – it is also important for children and youth. Providing financial education to children and youth can help set them up for long-term financial success by teaching them important financial skills and concepts at an early age.

Financial education is a lifelong process. Financial concepts and strategies are constantly evolving, and it is important for individuals to continue learning and staying informed about the latest developments in personal finance.

The Wealth mindset

In conclusion, financial education and literacy are critical for promoting long-term financial security, breaking the cycle of poverty, promoting economic equality, and protecting individuals from financial scams and exploitation. By investing in financial education, we can help individuals make more informed financial decisions and build a more financially stable and secure future for themselves and their families.

Chapter 2

2.1 How to Expand Your Knowledge and Understanding of Money Management

Money management is a crucial life skill that is essential for everyone, regardless of their age, profession, or income level. Unfortunately, financial literacy is not taught in most schools, and many people lack the knowledge and skills required to manage their finances effectively. This lack of financial education can lead to poor financial decisions, debt, and financial insecurity. However, with a little effort, anyone can expand their knowledge and understanding of money management. In this article, we will discuss some practical tips for how to expand your knowledge of money management.

2.2 Read books on personal finance:

There are countless books on personal finance available that cover everything from budgeting and saving to investing and retirement planning. Reading books on personal finance is an excellent way to gain a solid understanding of the basics of money management. Some popular titles include "The Total Money Makeover" by Dave Ramsey, "Rich Dad Poor Dad" by Robert Kiyosaki, and "The Intelligent Investor" by Benjamin Graham.

2.3 Take online courses:

Many reputable online platforms offer courses on personal finance, investing, and money management. These courses are usually self-paced and can be completed from the comfort of your own home. Some popular platforms that offer personal finance courses include Coursera, Udemy, and Skill share.

2.4 Attend financial workshops or seminars:

Many organizations, including banks and community centers, offer financial workshops and seminars on a variety of topics related to money management. These workshops are usually led by financial experts and can be an excellent opportunity to learn from professionals and ask questions.

2.5 Join a financial book club or discussion group:

Joining a financial book club or discussion group can be an excellent way to learn from others and exchange ideas about money management. These groups can be found online or in person, and they offer an opportunity to discuss personal finance topics with like-minded individuals.

2.6 Subscribe to financial newsletters and podcasts:

Many financial experts and organizations offer free newsletters and podcasts that cover personal finance topics. These newsletters and podcasts can be a great way to stay up-to-date on the latest trends and developments in the world of finance.

2.7 Seek advice from financial professionals:

If you have specific questions or concerns about your finances, it may be helpful to seek advice from a financial professional. Financial advisors, accountants, and other professionals can provide valuable insight and guidance on money management and financial planning.

2.8 Practice what you learn:

Finally, the best way to expand your knowledge of money management is to put what you learn into practice. Set financial goals, create a budget, start investing, and track your progress. By taking action, you will gain practical experience and build confidence in your ability to manage your finances effectively.

2.9 Follow financial experts and influencers:

Follow financial experts and influencers on social media or through their blogs to stay up-to-date on the latest trends and tips in money management. Some popular financial experts include Suze Orman, Dave Ramsey, and Robert Kiyosaki.

2.10 Use financial management tools:

There are numerous financial management tools available that can help you track your spending, create a budget, and manage your investments. Some popular tools include Mint, Personal Capital, and Quicken.

In conclusion, expanding your knowledge of money management is an essential step towards achieving financial security and independence. By reading books, taking courses, attending workshops, joining groups, subscribing to newsletters and podcasts, seeking advice from professionals, and practicing what you learn, you can develop a strong foundation of financial literacy and set yourself up for success.

Chapter 3

3.1 The Basics of Personal Finance, Investing, and Wealth Building

Personal finance, investing, and wealth building are important areas of knowledge for anyone who wants to take control of their financial future. By understanding these basics, individuals can make informed decisions about their money, save for their goals, and build wealth over time.

Personal finance encompasses a wide range of topics, including budgeting, saving, debt management, and retirement planning. To get started with personal finance, it's important to first understand your current financial situation. This includes taking stock of your income, expenses, debts, and assets. Once you have a clear understanding of your financial picture, you can begin to create a budget that works for you.

Budgeting involves creating a plan for how you will spend your money each month. This can include setting aside money for bills, savings, and discretionary spending. A budget helps you to stay on track with your financial goals and can help you avoid overspending.

Savings are a critical component of personal finance. Setting aside money for an emergency fund and retirement are two key areas to focus on. An emergency fund provides a financial cushion for unexpected expenses, such as a medical emergency or a car repair.

Retirement savings are important for long-term financial security and should be started as early as possible.

Debt management is also an important aspect of personal finance. If you have debt, it's important to create a plan for paying it off. This may involve prioritizing high-interest debt, such as credit card debt, and making extra payments to reduce the balance.

Investing is a way to put your money to work for you. By investing in stocks, bonds, mutual funds, and other assets, you have the potential to earn a return on your investment over time. Investing does come with some risk, however, and it's important to understand the potential risks and rewards before investing your money.

Wealth building involves creating a long-term plan for building wealth over time. This can involve a combination of savings, debt management, and investing. A key component of wealth building is creating a diversified investment portfolio that balances risk and reward.

To expand your knowledge and understanding of personal finance, investing, and wealth building, there are a number of resources available. These include books, online courses, podcasts, and financial advisors. It's important to do your research and choose resources that align with your financial goals and values.

In addition to these basics, there are some important principles to keep in mind when it comes to personal finance, investing, and wealth building. These include:

3.2 Start early:

The earlier you start saving and investing, the more time your money has to grow. Starting early also allows you to take advantage of compound interest, which can have a significant impact on your long-term wealth.

3.3 Diversify:

Diversifying your investments can help to reduce risk and maximize returns. This involves spreading your money across different asset classes, such as stocks, bonds, and real estate.

3.4 Be patient:

Building wealth takes time and patience. It's important to have a long-term perspective and avoid making impulsive decisions based on short-term market fluctuations.

3.5 Keep costs low:

Fees and expenses can eat into your investment returns over time. It's important to choose low-cost investments and avoid unnecessary fees whenever possible.

3.6 Stay informed:

Staying informed about the markets and your investments is important for making informed decisions.

This includes keeping up with financial news, reviewing your investment portfolio regularly, and staying in touch with a financial advisor or mentor.

3.7 Retirement planning:

It's important to start planning for retirement early in your career to ensure that you have enough money saved up to maintain your lifestyle after you stop working.

3.8 Debt management:

Understanding how to manage debt is crucial to maintaining good financial health. This includes knowing how to pay off high-interest debt, such as credit card balances, and avoiding unnecessary debt.

3.9 Real estate investing:

Investing in real estate can be a great way to build wealth, but it's important to understand the risks involved and to do your due diligence before making any investments.

3.10 Tax planning:

Knowing how to minimize your tax liability can help you keep more of your hard-earned money. This includes understanding deductions, credits, and tax-advantaged investment accounts.

3.11 Estate planning:

Estate planning involves creating a plan for how your assets will be distributed after you pass away. It's important to consider factors such as estate taxes, probate, and guardianship of minor children.

3.12 Behavioral finance:

Behavioral finance is the study of how psychological biases and emotions can influence financial decisions. Understanding these biases can help you make better decisions and avoid common pitfalls.

3.13 Philanthropy:

Giving back to your community or supporting causes that are important to you can be a fulfilling part of your financial plan. Understanding the different ways to give, such as charitable trusts or donor-advised funds, can help you maximize the impact of your giving.

3.14 Alternative investments:

Alternative investments, such as hedge funds, private equity, or commodities, can provide diversification and potentially higher returns, but they also come with higher risk. Understanding the pros and cons of alternative investments can help you make informed decisions.

3.15 Entrepreneurship:

Starting your own business can be a great way to build wealth, but it also comes with significant risks. Understanding the basics of entrepreneurship, including business planning, financing, and marketing, can help you increase your chances of success.

3.16 Global investing:

With the increasing globalization of financial markets, it's important to understand the risks and opportunities of investing in international markets. This includes understanding currency risk, political risk, and cultural differences.

By following these principles and continuing to learn about personal finance, investing, and wealth building, you can take control of your financial future and build long-term wealth over time.

Chapter 4

4.1 Common Financial Mistakes to Avoid

When it comes to personal finance, mistakes can be costly and have long-term effects on your financial well-being. Even the most financially savvy individuals can make errors in judgment or fall victim to common pitfalls. Here are some common financial mistakes to avoid:

4.2 Overspending:

Overspending is one of the most common financial mistakes people make. It's easy to get caught up in the moment and spend more than you can afford. This can lead to debt, high interest rates, and financial stress. It's important to create a budget and stick to it, avoiding unnecessary expenses and impulse purchases.

4.3 Failing to save:

Saving is critical to achieving long-term financial goals, such as retirement, buying a house, or starting a business. Failing to save can put you in a precarious financial position and limit your opportunities. It's important to make saving a priority, even if it means making sacrifices in the short-term.

4.4 Neglecting retirement planning:

Many people fail to plan for retirement or don't start saving early enough. This can lead to a significant shortfall in retirement savings, making it difficult to maintain your standard of living in your golden years. It's important to start planning and saving for retirement as early as possible, even if it's just a small amount each month.

4.5 Not having an emergency fund:

Unexpected expenses can arise at any time, such as medical bills or car repairs. Without an emergency fund, you may be forced to rely on credit cards or loans to cover these expenses, which can lead to debt and financial stress. It's important to have an emergency fund to cover at least 3-6 months of expenses.

4.6 Carrying credit card debt:

Credit card debt can be a significant burden, with high interest rates and fees. Carrying a balance from month to month can make it difficult to get ahead financially, as your payments go primarily toward interest rather than paying down the principal. It's important to pay off credit card balances in full each month to avoid interest charges and fees.

4.7 Not monitoring credit score:

Your credit score is a critical component of your financial health, as it impacts your ability to borrow money, get approved for credit cards, and even rent an apartment or get a job. Failing to monitor your credit score can lead to errors or inaccuracies that can hurt your creditworthiness. It's important to monitor your credit score regularly and correct any errors.

4.8 Ignoring insurance needs:

Insurance is a critical part of financial planning, protecting you and your assets from unexpected events. Failing to have adequate insurance coverage, such as health, auto, or homeowners insurance, can leave you vulnerable to significant financial losses. It's important to review your insurance needs regularly and ensure you have adequate coverage.

4.9 Investing without a plan:

Investing can be an effective way to grow your wealth, but it's important to have a plan and understand the risks involved. Investing without a plan can lead to poor investment decisions or taking on too much risk. It's important to develop an investment plan that aligns with your financial goals and risk tolerance.

4.10 Neglecting estate planning:

Estate planning is critical to ensuring your assets are distributed according to your wishes and that your loved ones are taken care of in the event of your death. Failing to have a will or trust can lead to legal battles and family disputes, making an already difficult time even more challenging. It's important to have an estate plan in place, including a will, power of attorney, and health care directive.

4.11 Failing to seek professional advice:

Personal finance can be complex, and it's easy to make mistakes or overlook important details. Failing to seek professional advice, such as from a financial advisor, accountant, or attorney, can lead to costly mistakes or missed opportunities.

4.12 Not having an emergency fund:

Life is unpredictable, and unexpected expenses can come up at any time. It is important to have an emergency fund to cover these expenses so that you do not have to rely on credit cards or loans.

4.13 Not having a budget:

Without a budget, it is easy to overspend and not know where your money is going. Creating and sticking to a budget is crucial for financial success.

4.14 Living beyond your means:

It can be tempting to want to keep up with friends or peers who have a higher income, but living beyond your means can lead to debt and financial stress. It is important to live within your means and only spend what you can afford.

4.15 Not saving for retirement:

Retirement may seem far off, but it is important to start saving as early as possible. Not saving enough for retirement can lead to financial struggles later in life.

4.16 Taking on too much debt:

While some debt, such as a mortgage or student loans, may be necessary, taking on too much debt can be detrimental to your financial health. It is important to avoid unnecessary debt and pay off existing debt as soon as possible.

4.17 Not having insurance:

Insurance is a way to protect yourself from financial losses due to unforeseen events, such as illness or accidents. Not having insurance can lead to significant financial strain if these events occur.

4.18 Not investing:

Investing is a way to grow your wealth over time, but not investing at all can lead to missed opportunities for financial growth. It is important to educate yourself about investing and start investing as early as possible.

4.19 Making emotional financial decisions:

Financial decisions should be made based on facts and logic, not emotions. Making decisions based on fear, greed, or other emotions can lead to poor financial outcomes.

4.20 Not seeking professional financial advice:

It can be difficult to navigate the world of personal finance on your own. Seeking professional financial advice can help you make informed decisions and avoid costly mistakes.

4.21 Not regularly reviewing and adjusting your financial plan:

Financial goals and circumstances can change over time, and it is important to regularly review and adjust your financial plan to ensure that you are on track to meet your goals.

In conclusion, financial education and literacy are crucial in building wealth and achieving financial success. By expanding your knowledge of money management, personal finance, and investing, you can make informed decisions and avoid common financial mistakes. It is also essential to develop a mindset of abundance and generosity, as well as to surround yourself with positive influences and build a support system of like-minded individuals. Overcoming fear and anxiety in networking and social situations and cultivating emotional intelligence are also key to achieving success in all aspects of life, including finance. Remember, the journey to financial success is a continuous process, and setbacks and obstacles will arise along the way. However, by staying focused, motivated, and adaptable, you can overcome these challenges and achieve your financial goals.

Chapter 5

5.1 Developing a Financial Plan and Strategy

Developing a financial plan and strategy is an important step in achieving your financial goals. A financial plan can help you organize your finances, prioritize your goals, and make informed decisions about your money. It can also help you track your progress and adjust your strategies as needed.

Here are some key steps to developing a financial plan and strategy:

5.2 Set Financial Goals:

Before you can develop a plan, you need to identify your financial goals. These may include short-term goals like paying off debt, long-term goals like saving for retirement, or a combination of both.

5.3 Assess Your Current Financial Situation:

Once you've identified your goals, it's important to assess your current financial situation. This includes taking stock of your income, expenses, assets, and debts. Understanding where you stand financially can help you identify areas for improvement and set realistic goals.

5.4 Create a Budget:

A budget is a crucial tool for managing your finances. It can help you track your expenses, prioritize your spending, and ensure that you're living within your means. To create a budget, start by tracking your income and expenses for a month. Then, identify areas where you can cut back and set spending limits for different categories.

5.5 Develop a Savings Plan:

Saving money is an essential part of any financial plan. Once you've created a budget, identify areas where you can save money and set savings goals. This may include building an emergency fund, saving for a down payment on a home, or contributing to a retirement account.

5.6 Manage Your Debt:

Managing your debt is a key component of any financial plan. Start by making a plan to pay off any high-interest debt, such as credit card debt. Then, consider strategies for managing other types of debt, such as student loans or a mortgage.

5.7 Invest for the Future:

Investing can help you grow your wealth over time. Consider working with a financial advisor to develop an investment strategy that aligns with your goals and risk tolerance.

5.8 Review and Adjust Your Plan:

A financial plan is not set in stone. It's important to regularly review your plan and make adjustments as needed. This may include adjusting your budget, increasing your savings goals, or rebalancing your investment portfolio.

5.9 Set clear and specific goals:

To create an effective financial plan, it's important to define your goals in a clear and specific way. This includes setting realistic timelines for achieving those goals, as well as determining the steps you need to take to get there.

5.10 Assess your current financial situation:

Before you can develop a financial plan, you need to know where you stand financially. This means taking a close look at your income, expenses, assets, and liabilities. From there, you can identify areas where you can cut back on spending or increase your income, as well as potential investments or assets to leverage.

5.11 Create a budget:

A budget is a critical component of any financial plan. It allows you to track your income and expenses and make adjustments as needed to stay on track towards your financial goals. Be sure to create a realistic budget that accounts for all of your expenses, including debt payments, savings, and discretionary spending.

5.12 Plan for emergencies:

Unexpected expenses can quickly derail even the most well-crafted financial plan. To account for this, it's important to set aside a portion of your income in an emergency fund. This can help cover unexpected expenses without derailing your progress towards your long-term financial goals.

5.13 Develop a debt repayment plan:

Debt can be a significant barrier to financial freedom, so it's important to have a plan in place for paying it off. This may involve prioritizing high-interest debt first, negotiating with creditors for lower interest rates or repayment terms, or consolidating multiple debts into a single loan.

5.14 Maximize your savings:

Saving money is an important aspect of any financial plan, and there are a variety of ways to maximize your savings. This may include contributing to a retirement account, opening a high-yield savings account, or investing in stocks, bonds, or other assets.

5.15 Revisit and adjust your plan as needed:

A financial plan is not set in stone and should be revisited and adjusted as your circumstances change. This may involve adjusting your budget, reallocating investments, or reassessing your financial goals.

In conclusion, developing a financial plan and strategy is an important step in achieving your financial goals. By setting goals, assessing your current financial situation, creating a budget, developing a savings plan, managing your debt, investing for the future, and regularly reviewing and adjusting your plan, you can take control of your finances and build a solid foundation for your financial future.

Chapter 6

6.1 How to Maximize Your Income and Earnings Potential

As humans, we all have desires and aspirations, and achieving them often requires money. Therefore, it's essential to set financial goals to maximize your income and earnings potential. In this chapter, I will explore why setting financial goals is critical and how it can impact your earning potential.

6.2 The Importance of Setting Financial Goals:

Firstly, setting financial goals helps you prioritize your spending and investment decisions. When you know what you want to achieve financially, you can focus your energy and resources on activities that will help you reach those goals. This approach helps you avoid spending money on things that don't contribute to your financial success, such as frivolous expenses or impulsive purchases.

Secondly, setting financial goals provides clarity and motivation. When you have a clear target, it's easier to measure your progress and celebrate your accomplishments. This approach provides the momentum you need to stay motivated, especially during challenging times when your financial progress may be slow.

Finally, setting financial goals helps you maximize your income and earnings potential. When you know what you want to achieve financially, you can identify opportunities to increase your income and optimize your financial decisions. This approach ensures that you're making informed decisions that align with your financial goals.

In summary, setting financial goals is a critical step in maximizing your income and earnings potential. In the next chapter, we'll explore how to set financial goals that are specific, measurable, achievable, relevant, and time-bound (SMART goals).

6.3 Setting SMART Financial Goals:

Now that you understand the importance of setting financial goals, it's time to learn how to set SMART financial goals. SMART is an acronym for Specific, Measurable, Achievable, Relevant, and Time-bound. When you set SMART financial goals, you increase your chances of achieving them and maximizing your income and earnings potential.

6.4 Specific:

Your financial goals should be specific and clearly defined. For example, instead of setting a vague goal of "making more money," set a specific goal of "earning an additional $10,000 in the next 12 months."

6.5 Measurable:

Your financial goals should be measurable so that you can track your progress and determine whether you're making progress towards achieving your goals. For example, instead of setting a goal of "saving more money," set a measurable goal of "saving $500 per month for the next 6 months."

6.6 Achievable:

Your financial goals should be achievable and within your control. Avoid setting goals that are too ambitious or unrealistic. For example, if you earn $50,000 per year, setting a goal of earning $1 million in the next 12 months is not achievable.

6.7 Relevant:

Your financial goals should be relevant to your overall financial plan and aspirations. For example, if your goal is to save for a down payment on a home, your financial goals should align with this objective.

6.8 Time-bound:

Your financial goals should have a deadline or timeframe. Setting a deadline provides a sense of urgency and helps you stay focused. For example, instead of setting a goal of "paying off debt," set a time-bound goal of "paying off $10,000 in credit card debt in the next 12 months."

In summary, setting SMART financial goals is an effective way to maximize your income and earnings potential. In the next chapter, we'll explore how to create a budget that aligns with your financial goals and helps you achieve them.

6.9 Creating a Budget to Maximize Your Income and Earnings Potential:

Now that you've set SMART financial goals, it's time to create a budget that aligns with those goals and helps you achieve them. A budget is a financial plan that outlines your income, expenses, and savings. Creating a budget is an essential step in maximizing your income and earnings potential.

Start by tracking your income and expenses for at least a month. This approach will help you understand your spending habits and identify areas where you can reduce your expenses. Once you have a clear picture of your income and expenses, create a budget that includes your SMART financial goals.

6.10 Your budget should include the following categories:

Fixed Expenses:

These are expenses that don't change from month to month, such as rent or mortgage payments, car payments, or insurance premiums.

Variable Expenses:

These are expenses that fluctuate from month to month, such as groceries, utilities, or entertainment expenses.

Savings:

This category includes contributions to your retirement accounts, emergency fund, or other savings goals.

Debt Repayment:

If you have any outstanding debts, such as credit card debt or student loans, include a category for debt repayment in your budget.

Once you have your budget in place, review it regularly to ensure that you're staying on track towards achieving your financial goals. Make adjustments as necessary, especially if your income or expenses change.

In summary, creating a budget is an essential step in maximizing your income and earnings potential. By tracking your income and expenses, setting SMART financial goals, and aligning your budget with those goals, you can take control of your finances and achieve financial success. In the next chapter, we'll explore how to increase your income and earnings potential through career development and side hustles.

Chapter 7

7.1 Strategies for Reducing Debt and Managing Your Finances Wisely

Managing finances can be a challenging task for many people. One of the biggest financial burdens that people face is debt. Debt can be a major obstacle to achieving financial freedom and can cause stress and anxiety. However, there are several strategies that you can use to reduce debt and manage your finances wisely. In this article, we will explore some of these strategies in detail.

7.2 Create a Budget:

The first step to managing your finances is to create a budget. A budget is a plan that outlines your income and expenses. It helps you to understand how much money you have coming in and going out each month. Creating a budget can be a daunting task, but it is essential for managing your finances effectively.

To create a budget, start by listing all of your income sources. This may include your salary, rental income, or any other sources of income. Next, list all of your expenses. This may include rent/mortgage, utilities, groceries, transportation, and entertainment expenses. Be sure to include all expenses, no matter how small.

Once you have listed all of your income and expenses, subtract your total expenses from your total income. If you have a surplus, this can be put towards paying off debt or building up savings. If you have a deficit, you may need to cut back on expenses or find ways to increase your income.

7.3 Cut Back on Expenses:

Cutting back on expenses is an effective way to reduce debt and manage your finances wisely. There are several ways to cut back on expenses. One way is to reduce your discretionary spending. This may include eating out less, canceling subscriptions you don't use, or finding cheaper alternatives to your current expenses.

Another way to cut back on expenses is to negotiate your bills. For example, you can call your utility provider and ask for a lower rate or switch to a cheaper provider. You can also negotiate your cable or internet bill or shop around for cheaper insurance rates.

7.4 Increase Your Income:

Increasing your income is another effective way to manage your finances and reduce debt. There are several ways to increase your income. One way is to ask for a raise at work. If you are self-employed, you can increase your prices or take on more clients.

Another way to increase your income is to sell items you no longer need. You can sell items online or have a garage sale. You can also offer services such as pet sitting or lawn care to earn extra income.

7.5 Prioritize Debt Repayment:

Prioritizing debt repayment is essential for reducing debt and managing your finances wisely. There are two common strategies for prioritizing debt repayment: the debt snowball and the debt avalanche.

The debt snowball method involves paying off your smallest debt first while making minimum payments on your other debts. Once the smallest debt is paid off, you move on to the next smallest debt and continue until all of your debts are paid off.

The debt avalanche method involves paying off your debt with the highest interest rate first while making minimum payments on your other debts. Once the debt with the highest interest rate is paid off, you move on to the next highest interest rate debt and continue until all of your debts are paid off.

7.6 Consolidate Debt:

Consolidating debt can be an effective way to reduce debt and manage your finances. Consolidating debt involves taking out a loan to pay off multiple debts. This can simplify your debt repayment by consolidating multiple payments into one payment with a lower interest rate.

There are several ways to consolidate debt. One way is to take out a personal loan. Another way is to use a balance transfer credit card. Balance transfer credit cards offer a 0% introductory APR for a limited time, allowing you to transfer your high-interest debt to the card and pay it off interest-free.

7.7 Build an Emergency Fund:

Building an emergency fund is an essential component of managing your finances wisely. An emergency fund is a savings account that is dedicated to covering unexpected expenses such as car repairs, medical bills, or job loss. Having an emergency fund can help you avoid going into debt when unexpected expenses arise.

To build an emergency fund, start by setting a savings goal. Aim to save three to six months' worth of living expenses. Next, automate your savings by setting up a recurring transfer from your checking account to your savings account each month. Consider opening a high-yield savings account to earn a higher interest rate on your savings.

7.8 Avoid Taking on New Debt:

Avoiding taking on new debt is crucial for reducing debt and managing your finances wisely. This means avoiding using credit cards to finance purchases that you cannot afford to pay off in full each month. It also means avoiding taking out new loans or lines of credit unless it is absolutely necessary.

One way to avoid taking on new debt is to create a budget and stick to it. This can help you identify areas where you can cut back on expenses and avoid using credit cards to finance purchases. Another way to avoid taking on new debt is to build an emergency fund. Having an emergency fund can help you cover unexpected expenses without relying on credit cards or loans.

7.9 Seek Professional Help:

If you are struggling to manage your finances or reduce your debt, seeking professional help can be beneficial. A financial advisor can help you create a budget, prioritize debt repayment, and develop a long-term financial plan. They can also provide guidance on investment strategies and retirement planning.

If you are struggling with debt, consider working with a credit counselor. A credit counselor can help you develop a debt repayment plan and negotiate with creditors to reduce interest rates or payment amounts. They can also provide guidance on budgeting and managing your finances.

In conclusion, managing your finances and reducing debt can be a challenging task, but it is essential for achieving financial freedom and reducing stress and anxiety. By creating a budget, cutting back on expenses, increasing your income, prioritizing debt repayment, consolidating debt, building an emergency fund, avoiding taking on new debt, and seeking professional help when necessary, you can take control of your finances and achieve your financial goals.

7.10 Consider Debt Consolidation:

If you have multiple high-interest debts, such as credit cards or personal loans, consolidating them into a single loan with a lower interest rate can make it easier to manage your debt and reduce your overall interest costs. Debt consolidation can be done through a balance transfer credit card, a personal loan, or a home equity loan or line of credit.

Before consolidating your debts, it's important to do your research and compare interest rates and fees from different lenders. You should also consider any potential drawbacks, such as a longer repayment term or the risk of putting your home at risk if you use a home equity loan.

7.11 Review Your Credit Report:

Your credit report is a record of your credit history and is used by lenders to evaluate your creditworthiness. Reviewing your credit report regularly can help you identify any errors or inaccuracies that could be negatively impacting your credit score.

You can obtain a free copy of your credit report from each of the three major credit bureaus (Equifax, Experian, and TransUnion) once a year at annualcreditreport.com. Review your report carefully and dispute any errors or inaccuracies with the credit bureau.

Maintaining a good credit score is important for managing your finances wisely because it can impact your ability to obtain credit, secure a loan, or get a job.

7.12 Stay Motivated and Track Your Progress:

Reducing debt and managing your finances wisely can be a long and challenging journey. To stay motivated, set specific goals and track your progress regularly. Celebrate small victories along the way and remind yourself of why you are making the effort to improve your financial situation.

Consider using a budgeting app or spreadsheet to track your expenses, income, and debt repayment progress. Seeing the numbers and graphs can help you stay focused and motivated.

7.13 Conclusion:

Managing your finances and reducing debt requires discipline, patience, and commitment. By creating a budget, cutting back on expenses, increasing your income, prioritizing debt repayment, consolidating debt, building an emergency fund, avoiding taking on new debt, seeking professional help when necessary, considering debt consolidation, reviewing your credit report, and staying motivated, you can take control of your finances and achieve your financial goals. Remember, managing your finances is a lifelong journey, so be patient, stay focused, and never give up.

Chapter 8

8.1 How to Build a Diverse and Balanced Investment Portfolio

Building a diverse and balanced investment portfolio is crucial for achieving long-term financial success. An investment portfolio is a collection of assets, such as stocks, bonds, and real estate, that are designed to help investors achieve their financial goals. A well-diversified and balanced portfolio can help investors minimize risk and maximize returns.

In this article, we will discuss the key steps for building a diverse and balanced investment portfolio.

8.2 Determine Your Investment Objectives and Risk Tolerance:

Before building your investment portfolio, it is important to determine your investment objectives and risk tolerance. Your investment objectives will depend on your financial goals, such as retirement, buying a house, or saving for a child's education. Your risk tolerance will depend on your willingness to take on risk and your ability to tolerate losses.

Investors with a higher risk tolerance may be more willing to invest in higher-risk assets, such as stocks, while investors with a lower risk tolerance may prefer to invest in lower-risk assets, such as bonds.

8.3 Allocate Your Assets:

Once you have determined your investment objectives and risk tolerance, it is time to allocate your assets. Asset allocation is the process of dividing your portfolio among different asset classes, such as stocks, bonds, and real estate.

The ideal asset allocation will depend on your investment objectives and risk tolerance. For example, if you have a higher risk tolerance and a long-term investment horizon, you may want to allocate a higher percentage of your portfolio to stocks. On the other hand, if you have a lower risk tolerance and a shorter investment horizon, you may want to allocate a higher percentage of your portfolio to bonds.

A common rule of thumb for asset allocation is the 60/40 rule, which recommends allocating 60% of your portfolio to stocks and 40% to bonds.

8.4 Diversify Your Portfolio:

Once you have allocated your assets, it is important to diversify your portfolio. Diversification is the process of spreading your investments across different industries, sectors, and geographies. This can help reduce risk by ensuring that your portfolio is not overly exposed to any one asset or market.

There are several ways to diversify your portfolio, including:

Investing in different asset classes:

By investing in different asset classes, such as stocks, bonds, and real estate, you can reduce risk and maximize returns.

Investing in different industries and sectors:

By investing in different industries and sectors, you can reduce risk by ensuring that your portfolio is not overly exposed to any one industry or sector.

Investing in different geographies:

By investing in different geographies, you can reduce risk by ensuring that your portfolio is not overly exposed to any one country or region.

Investing in different types of securities:

By investing in different types of securities, such as stocks, bonds, and mutual funds, you can reduce risk by ensuring that your portfolio is not overly exposed to any one type of security.

8.5 Rebalance Your Portfolio:

Once you have built your investment portfolio, it is important to regularly review and rebalance your portfolio. Rebalancing involves adjusting your portfolio to ensure that it remains aligned with your investment objectives and risk tolerance.

For example, if your investment objectives change, you may need to adjust your asset allocation to reflect your new goals. Similarly, if your risk tolerance changes, you may need to adjust your asset allocation to reflect your new risk tolerance.

Rebalancing can help ensure that your portfolio remains diversified and balanced, and can help maximize returns while minimizing risk.

8.6 Monitor Your Portfolio:

Finally, it is important to monitor your investment portfolio on a regular basis. This can involve reviewing your portfolio performance, tracking your investments, and staying up-to-date on market trends and news.

By monitoring your portfolio, you can identify any changes in your investments or the market that may require adjustments to your portfolio. This can help you make informed decisions about your investments and ensure that your portfolio remains aligned with your investment objectives and risk tolerance.

Additionally, monitoring your portfolio can help you identify opportunities for growth and maximize returns. For example, if you notice that one of your investments is performing particularly well, you may consider increasing your allocation to that investment to capitalize on its growth potential.

In conclusion, building a diverse and balanced investment portfolio is a key component of achieving long-term financial success. By following these steps, investors can create a portfolio that is aligned with their investment objectives and risk tolerance, diversified across different asset classes and securities, and regularly monitored and rebalanced to ensure optimal performance. By taking a thoughtful and strategic approach to investing, investors can minimize risk and maximize returns, and achieve their financial goals over the long term.

Chapter 9

9.1 The Connection Between Giving Back and Financial Success

The connection between giving back and financial success is a topic that has been debated for decades. Some people believe that the more you give, the more you receive, while others think that giving back has no direct impact on financial success. However, research and personal experiences have shown that there is a strong correlation between giving back and financial success.

Giving back is not just about donating money to charity. It can also include volunteering time, sharing knowledge, and providing mentorship to others. When people give back, they are contributing to their community and making a positive impact on the world. In return, they often receive intangible benefits, such as a sense of purpose, fulfillment, and personal growth.

The idea that giving back can lead to financial success is rooted in the concept of karma, which is the idea that your actions determine your future. According to karma, if you do good things, good things will happen to you, and if you do bad things, bad things will happen to you. While this idea may seem mystical, there is a scientific basis for it.

Studies have shown that when people give back, they experience a release of dopamine, which is a neurotransmitter that is associated with pleasure and reward. This release of dopamine can lead to a positive feedback loop, where people feel good about themselves and are more likely to continue giving back. Additionally, when people give back, they often build social connections and networks that can lead to new opportunities and financial success.

Furthermore, giving back can help people develop important skills that are highly valued in the business world. For example, volunteering can provide opportunities for leadership, teamwork, and communication, which are all essential skills in any profession. Additionally, providing mentorship to others can help people develop their own leadership and coaching skills, which can be highly sought after in the business world.

Giving back can also help people build a strong reputation and personal brand. When people give back, they are demonstrating their values and their commitment to making a positive impact on the world. This can help them build a strong reputation as a leader and an influencer, which can open up new opportunities for career advancement and financial success.

Moreover, giving back can also help people develop a sense of empathy and compassion, which are essential qualities for effective leadership. When people are able to understand and connect with others on a deep level, they are more likely to be able to inspire and motivate them towards a common goal. This can lead to greater success in the workplace and in other areas of life.

In conclusion, there is a strong connection between giving back and financial success. When people give back, they are contributing to their community and making a positive impact on the world. This can lead to a release of dopamine, which can create a positive feedback loop and lead to continued giving back. Additionally, giving back can help people develop important skills, build a strong reputation, and develop a sense of empathy and compassion, all of which are highly valued in the business world. Ultimately, giving back is not just about doing good, it is also about creating opportunities for personal and financial success.

Moreover, giving back can also lead to the creation of new business opportunities. When people give back, they often build relationships with other like-minded individuals, who may be potential business partners, clients, or investors. By demonstrating their commitment to making a positive impact, they may attract others who share their values and want to work with them to create change.

Furthermore, giving back can also lead to increased customer loyalty and brand loyalty. Consumers are increasingly looking for companies that are socially responsible and give back to their communities. By demonstrating a commitment to social responsibility, companies can attract and retain customers who are looking for brands that align with their values. This can lead to increased revenue and profitability in the long run.

In addition to the benefits for individuals and companies, giving back can also have a positive impact on society as a whole. When people give back, they are contributing to the common good and helping to create a more equitable and just society. This can lead to a more stable and prosperous society, which can benefit everyone, including those who may be struggling financially.

Overall, the connection between giving back and financial success is clear. Giving back can lead to a release of dopamine, which can create a positive feedback loop and lead to continued giving back. It can also help people develop important skills, build a strong reputation, and develop a sense of empathy and compassion, all of which are highly valued in the business world. Moreover, giving back can lead to new business opportunities, increased customer and brand loyalty, and a more stable and prosperous society. Therefore, it is important for individuals and companies to prioritize giving back and making a positive impact on the world.

One important factor to consider when giving back is the concept of strategic philanthropy. Strategic philanthropy is the practice of using charitable donations and volunteer work to achieve specific social or environmental goals. By strategically investing in causes and organizations that align with their values and goals, individuals and companies can maximize the impact of their giving.

For example, a company that is committed to reducing its environmental footprint may choose to invest in a non-profit organization that promotes sustainable agriculture or renewable energy. By strategically investing in these causes, the company can not only make a positive impact on the environment but also enhance its reputation as a socially responsible business.

Similarly, individuals can also engage in strategic philanthropy by focusing their giving on causes that are aligned with their personal values and goals. For example, someone who is passionate about education may choose to donate to a non-profit organization that provides scholarships or educational resources to low-income students. By strategically investing in these causes, individuals can make a significant impact on the world while also gaining personal fulfillment and satisfaction.

It is also important to note that giving back should not be seen as a one-time event, but rather as a continuous practice. By integrating giving back into our daily lives and making it a part of our routine, we can create a positive habit that can lead to long-term impact and success.

In conclusion, the connection between giving back and financial success is strong, and it is important for individuals and companies to prioritize giving back and making a positive impact on the world. By strategically investing in causes and organizations that align with their values and goals, individuals and companies can maximize the impact of their giving and create a better world for everyone. Giving back is not only a way to do good but also a way to achieve personal and financial success.

Chapter 10

10.1 Tips for Maintaining Long-Term Financial Health and Security

Maintaining long-term financial health and security is an essential aspect of life. It allows you to live your life without worrying about your financial situation and focus on achieving your goals. Here are some tips to help you maintain long-term financial health and security.

10.2 Create a Budget and Stick to It:

The first step to maintaining long-term financial health and security is to create a budget. A budget helps you understand where your money is going and where you need to make changes to ensure you are saving and investing for the future. To create a budget, start by tracking your expenses for a month. This will help you see where your money is going and identify areas where you can cut back.

Once you have tracked your expenses, create a budget that includes all of your expenses, including your housing costs, food, transportation, entertainment, and other bills. Make sure you include savings and investment goals in your budget.

10.3 Save for Emergencies:

Unexpected expenses can put a dent in your finances and ruin your financial security. To protect yourself, create an emergency fund. An emergency fund is a savings account that you use to cover unexpected expenses, such as car repairs or medical bills.

A good rule of thumb is to have three to six months' worth of living expenses in your emergency fund. This will help you weather unexpected expenses without having to rely on credit cards or loans.

10.4 Pay Off High-Interest Debt:

High-interest debt can eat away at your finances and make it difficult to achieve long-term financial security. Make a plan to pay off high-interest debt, such as credit card debt or personal loans, as soon as possible.

Start by paying off the debt with the highest interest rate first. Then, once that debt is paid off, move on to the debt with the next highest interest rate.

10.5 Invest for the Future:

Investing is an important part of maintaining long-term financial health and security. Investing allows your money to grow over time, which can help you achieve your financial goals.

Start by investing in a retirement account, such as an IRA or 401(k). These accounts offer tax advantages and can help you save for retirement. You can also consider investing in stocks, mutual funds, or real estate.

10.6 Live Below Your Means:

Living below your means is a key part of maintaining long-term financial health and security. It means spending less than you earn and avoiding lifestyle inflation.

To live below your means, start by cutting back on unnecessary expenses. This could mean eating out less often, canceling subscriptions you don't use, or finding a cheaper place to live.

10.7 Build Multiple Streams of Income:

Having multiple streams of income can help you achieve long-term financial security. It means not relying on one source of income, such as a job, to meet all of your financial needs.

Consider starting a side hustle or freelancing to earn extra money. You can also invest in rental property or start a small business.

10.8 Protect Your Assets:

Protecting your assets is an important part of maintaining long-term financial health and security. This means having insurance to protect against unexpected events, such as car accidents or medical emergencies.

Make sure you have the appropriate insurance coverage for your needs, including health insurance, life insurance, and home or renters insurance.

10.9 Stay Informed:

Staying informed about financial news and trends is an important part of maintaining long-term financial health and security. Keep up-to-date with financial news by reading books, blogs, and news articles.

You can also work with a financial advisor to help you create a financial plan and make informed investment decisions.

10.10 Avoid Lifestyle Inflation:

Lifestyle inflation is the tendency to increase your spending as your income increases. This can make it difficult to save for the future and maintain long-term financial health and security.

To avoid lifestyle inflation, try to maintain the same standard of living even as your income increases. This means resisting the urge to upgrade your car, buy a bigger house, or take extravagant vacations.

Instead, focus on saving and investing your extra income to achieve your long-term financial goals.

10.11 Plan for Retirement:

Retirement planning is an essential part of maintaining long-term financial health and security. Start by estimating how much money you will need to retire comfortably.

Consider factors such as your current lifestyle, your expected expenses in retirement, and any retirement benefits you may receive from your employer or the government.

Once you have a target retirement savings amount, create a plan to save and invest for retirement. Consider working with a financial advisor to help you create a retirement plan that meets your needs.

10.12 Practice Good Credit Habits:

Maintaining good credit habits is important for long-term financial health and security. This means paying your bills on time, keeping your credit card balances low, and avoiding new debt.

Good credit habits can help you maintain a good credit score, which can make it easier to get approved for loans and credit cards in the future.

10.13 Review Your Finances Regularly:

Finally, it's important to review your finances regularly to ensure you are on track to achieve your long-term financial goals. This means checking your credit report, reviewing your budget, and monitoring your investment portfolio.

Regularly reviewing your finances can help you identify areas where you need to make changes to maintain long-term financial health and security.

In conclusion, maintaining long-term financial health and security requires discipline, planning, and commitment. By creating a budget, saving for emergencies, investing for the future, and practicing good credit habits, you can achieve financial freedom and peace of mind. Remember to stay informed, avoid lifestyle inflation, and review your finances regularly to ensure you stay on track to achieve your long-term financial goals.

Part 6 Complete

Part 7

Building a Support System

Success is rarely achieved alone. In this chapter, readers will learn about the importance of building a support system that encourages and supports their financial goals. The author will provide tips for finding and cultivating supportive relationships, both online and offline.

Chapter 1

1.1 The Importance of Maintaining a Positive and Healthy Lifestyle

A positive and healthy lifestyle is essential for maintaining good physical, emotional, and mental health. It involves making conscious decisions and choices that promote well-being and lead to a happier life. Maintaining a positive and healthy lifestyle requires discipline, motivation, and commitment. In this essay, we will discuss the importance of maintaining a positive and healthy lifestyle, its benefits, and ways to incorporate it into our daily lives.

1.2 Physical Health:

Physical health refers to the condition of our body and how well it functions. Maintaining a positive and healthy lifestyle has a significant impact on our physical health. It reduces the risk of chronic diseases such as heart disease, diabetes, and cancer. Engaging in regular exercise, eating a balanced diet, and getting enough sleep are essential for maintaining good physical health.

1.3 Exercise:

Regular exercise is crucial for maintaining physical health. It helps to improve cardiovascular health, strengthens muscles and bones, and reduces the risk of chronic diseases. Exercise releases endorphins, which are natural mood-boosters, making us feel happier and more energized. Incorporating physical activity into our daily routine can be as simple as taking a walk, going for a swim, or taking a yoga class.

1.4 Diet:

Eating a balanced diet is essential for maintaining good physical health. A healthy diet should consist of a variety of fruits, vegetables, lean proteins, and whole grains. Consuming too much sugar, salt, and saturated fats can lead to health problems such as obesity, high blood pressure, and high cholesterol levels. Drinking plenty of water is also essential for maintaining good physical health.

1.5 Sleep:

Getting enough sleep is crucial for maintaining physical health. Lack of sleep can lead to fatigue, irritability, and difficulty concentrating. It can also increase the risk of developing chronic diseases such as diabetes, heart disease, and obesity. The recommended amount of sleep for adults is 7-9 hours per night.

1.6 Emotional Health:

Emotional health refers to the state of our emotions and how we manage them. Maintaining a positive and healthy lifestyle has a significant impact on our emotional health. It helps to reduce stress, anxiety, and depression, and improves our overall well-being. Engaging in activities that we enjoy, socializing with others, and practicing mindfulness are essential for maintaining good emotional health.

1.7 Activities:

Engaging in activities that we enjoy can improve our emotional health. It helps to reduce stress, boost our mood, and improve our overall well-being. Activities can be anything from painting, reading, or dancing. It is essential to make time for activities that we enjoy, as it helps to reduce stress and improve our emotional health.

1.8 Socializing:

Socializing with others is crucial for maintaining good emotional health. It helps to reduce feelings of loneliness and isolation, and improves our overall well-being. Socializing can be anything from going out with friends, volunteering, or joining a club or group. It is essential to make time for socializing, as it helps to improve our emotional health.

1.9 Mindfulness:

Practicing mindfulness is essential for maintaining good emotional health. It helps to reduce stress, anxiety, and depression, and improves our overall well-being.

Mindfulness can be anything from meditation, yoga, or simply taking a few deep breaths. It is essential to make time for mindfulness, as it helps to improve our emotional health.

1.10 Mental Health:

Mental health refers to the state of our mind and how we think and feel. Maintaining a positive and healthy lifestyle has a significant impact on our mental health. It helps to reduce the risk of mental health problems such as depression, anxiety, and stress. Engaging in activities that challenge our mind, seeking support when needed, and practicing self-care are essential for maintaining good mental health.

1.11 Activities:

Engaging in activities that challenge our mind is essential for maintaining good mental health. It helps to improve cognitive function, memory, and concentration. Activities can be anything from reading, solving puzzles, or learning a new skill. It is essential to make time for activities that challenge our mind, as it helps to improve our mental health.

1.12 Seeking Support:

Seeking support when needed is crucial for maintaining good mental health. It is essential to seek professional help if we are experiencing symptoms of depression, anxiety, or stress. Talking to friends, family, or a counselor can also be beneficial for improving our mental health. It is important to remember that seeking support is a sign of strength, not weakness.

1.13 Self-Care:

Practicing self-care is essential for maintaining good mental health. It involves taking care of ourselves physically, emotionally, and mentally. Self-care can be anything from taking a relaxing bath, practicing meditation, or taking a day off work. It is essential to make time for self-care, as it helps to reduce stress and improve our mental health.

1.14 Benefits of Maintaining a Positive and Healthy Lifestyle:

Maintaining a positive and healthy lifestyle has numerous benefits. It improves our physical, emotional, and mental health, reduces the risk of chronic diseases, and improves our overall well-being. It also helps to improve our relationships with others, increase our productivity, and improve our quality of life.

1.15 Relationships:

Maintaining a positive and healthy lifestyle improves our relationships with others. It helps to reduce stress and improve communication skills, making it easier to connect with others. Engaging in activities that we enjoy with others can also help to strengthen our relationships.

1.16 Productivity:

Maintaining a positive and healthy lifestyle can increase our productivity. It improves our energy levels, concentration, and cognitive function, making it easier to accomplish tasks. Engaging in regular exercise can also improve our productivity, as it helps to improve our physical and mental health.

1.17 Quality of Life:

Maintaining a positive and healthy lifestyle improves our quality of life. It helps us to feel happier, more energetic, and more fulfilled. It also reduces the risk of chronic diseases, which can have a significant impact on our quality of life.

In addition to the benefits mentioned above, maintaining a positive and healthy lifestyle can also lead to a longer life. Studies have shown that individuals who engage in regular exercise, eat a healthy diet, and do not smoke or drink excessively, have a longer life expectancy than those who do not. This is because a healthy lifestyle can reduce the risk of chronic diseases such as heart disease, stroke, and diabetes.

Furthermore, maintaining a positive and healthy lifestyle can also lead to a more fulfilling life. When we take care of ourselves both physically and mentally, we are able to fully engage in and enjoy the activities that we love. We are also more likely to take on new challenges and try new things, which can lead to personal growth and development.

Another important aspect of maintaining a positive and healthy lifestyle is the impact it can have on our mental health. When we take care of our bodies, we also take care of our minds. Engaging in regular exercise, getting enough sleep, and practicing mindfulness can all help to reduce stress and anxiety, and improve our overall mental well-being.

It is also important to note that maintaining a positive and healthy lifestyle is not always easy. It requires discipline, commitment, and motivation. However, it is important to remember that the benefits are well worth the effort. Making small changes to our daily habits can have a significant impact on our overall well-being.

In conclusion, maintaining a positive and healthy lifestyle is essential for improving our physical, emotional, and mental health. It involves making conscious decisions and choices that promote well-being and lead to a happier life. Engaging in regular exercise, eating a balanced diet, getting enough sleep, socializing with others, practicing mindfulness, engaging in activities that challenge our mind, seeking support when needed, and practicing self-care are all essential for maintaining a positive and healthy lifestyle. The benefits of maintaining a positive and healthy lifestyle are numerous, including improving our relationships with others, increasing our productivity, and improving our quality of life.

Chapter 2

2.1 Strategies for Managing Stress and Overcoming Burnout

Stress is a common phenomenon that affects people of all ages, genders, and professions. It can be defined as a state of mental or emotional strain resulting from adverse or demanding circumstances. Burnout, on the other hand, is a type of stress that is specific to the workplace. It is characterized by feelings of exhaustion, cynicism, and a reduced sense of accomplishment. Burnout can occur in any profession, but it is most common in high-stress environments such as healthcare, education, and social work.

Stress and burnout have negative effects on individuals and organizations. They can lead to decreased productivity, increased absenteeism, and high turnover rates. Therefore, it is important to manage stress and overcome burnout to ensure personal and organizational success.

This article will provide strategies for managing stress and overcoming burnout. These strategies are based on scientific research and best practices in the field of psychology.

2.2 Understand the Causes of Stress and Burnout:

The first step in managing stress and overcoming burnout is to understand their causes. Stress can be caused by a variety of factors, including work demands, personal issues, and health problems. Burnout is specifically related to work-related stressors, such as a heavy workload, lack of control over work, and poor relationships with colleagues.

Understanding the causes of stress and burnout can help individuals and organizations to identify and address the root causes of these problems. For example, if an employee is experiencing stress due to a heavy workload, the organization can provide support by delegating tasks or hiring additional staff. If an employee is experiencing burnout due to poor relationships with colleagues, the organization can provide training on communication and conflict resolution.

2.3 Develop Coping Mechanisms:

The second strategy for managing stress and overcoming burnout is to develop coping mechanisms. Coping mechanisms are strategies that individuals use to deal with stress and difficult situations. There are two types of coping mechanisms: problem-focused coping and emotion-focused coping.

Problem-focused coping involves addressing the root cause of the stressor. This may involve developing a plan to address a difficult project or task, seeking support from colleagues or managers, or learning new skills to improve job performance. Emotion-focused coping involves managing the emotional response to stressors. This may involve engaging in relaxation techniques such as deep breathing or meditation, seeking social support, or engaging in enjoyable activities outside of work.

Developing coping mechanisms is an important part of managing stress and overcoming burnout. Coping mechanisms can help individuals to feel more in control of their situation, reduce negative emotions, and improve overall well-being.

2.4 Maintain a Healthy Lifestyle:

Maintaining a healthy lifestyle is another important strategy for managing stress and overcoming burnout. This includes getting enough sleep, eating a healthy diet, and engaging in regular exercise. Sleep is particularly important for managing stress and burnout as it allows the body to rest and recover. A lack of sleep can lead to increased stress and burnout, as well as other health problems such as obesity, diabetes, and heart disease.

Eating a healthy diet is also important for managing stress and burnout. A diet that is high in processed foods, sugar, and unhealthy fats can lead to fatigue, mood swings, and other health problems. On the other hand, a diet that is high in fruits, vegetables, whole grains, and lean protein can improve energy levels, mood, and overall health.

Regular exercise is also important for managing stress and burnout. Exercise has been shown to reduce stress, improve mood, and increase energy levels. Even a short walk or stretching session can provide benefits.

2.5 Set Boundaries:

Setting boundaries is an important strategy for managing stress and overcoming burnout. This involves setting limits on the amount of time and energy that is devoted to work and other activities. Setting boundaries can help individuals to prioritize their needs and responsibilities, and reduce the risk of burnout.

For example, setting boundaries may involve limiting work hours or taking regular breaks throughout the day. It may also involve saying no to additional responsibilities or delegating tasks to others. Setting boundaries can be difficult, especially in high-stress environments, but it is essential for maintaining a healthy work-life balance.

2.6 Practice Mindfulness:

Mindfulness is a practice that involves being fully present and aware of the present moment. It can be a powerful tool for managing stress and overcoming burnout. Mindfulness can help individuals to reduce stress, improve mood, and increase resilience.

There are many ways to practice mindfulness, including meditation, deep breathing, and yoga. It can also be practiced in daily activities, such as taking a walk or eating a meal. By focusing on the present moment and being aware of one's thoughts and emotions, individuals can gain a greater sense of control and reduce stress levels.

2.7 Seek Support:

Seeking support from colleagues, friends, or a mental health professional is an important strategy for managing stress and overcoming burnout. Talking to someone about one's feelings and concerns can provide a sense of relief and help individuals to gain perspective on their situation.

In addition, seeking support from a mental health professional can provide individuals with tools and strategies for managing stress and overcoming burnout. Therapy can help individuals to identify the root causes of their stress and develop coping mechanisms to manage it.

2.8 Take Time Off:

Taking time off is an important strategy for managing stress and overcoming burnout. This may include taking a vacation, a personal day, or a mental health day. Taking time off allows individuals to recharge and reset, and can help to reduce the risk of burnout.

Taking time off can be difficult, especially in high-stress environments where there may be pressure to work long hours or meet strict deadlines. However, it is essential for maintaining overall well-being and preventing burnout.

In conclusion, managing stress and overcoming burnout is essential for personal and organizational success. By understanding the causes of stress and burnout, developing coping mechanisms, maintaining a healthy lifestyle, setting boundaries, practicing mindfulness, seeking support, and taking time off, individuals can reduce stress levels, improve well-being, and increase resilience. It is important for individuals and organizations to prioritize mental health and well-being in order to achieve long-term success.

Chapter 3

3.1 Developing Healthy Habits and Routines to Support Your Wealth Mindset

A wealth mindset is not just about having a lot of money; it is about having a positive attitude towards money and using it to achieve your goals and dreams. Developing healthy habits and routines is essential to support a wealth mindset because it allows you to manage your finances effectively and make smart decisions about how to invest your money. In this article, we will explore the importance of developing healthy habits and routines to support a wealth mindset and provide tips for developing these habits.

3.2 Budgeting:

One of the most critical habits for supporting a wealth mindset is budgeting. Budgeting is the process of creating a plan for how you will spend your money. It helps you to prioritize your expenses and make sure you have enough money to cover your basic needs, while also allowing you to save and invest in your future.

To develop a budget, start by tracking your income and expenses for a few months. Use a budgeting app or spreadsheet to categorize your spending and identify areas where you can cut back. Then, create a budget that allocates your income towards your essential needs, savings, and investments.

3.3 Saving:

Saving is another critical habit for supporting a wealth mindset. By regularly setting aside a portion of your income, you can build up an emergency fund, save for big purchases, and invest in your future.

To start saving, set a goal for how much you want to save each month and make it a priority. Consider setting up automatic transfers from your checking account to your savings account to ensure you stay on track.

3.4 Investing:

Investing is a powerful tool for growing your wealth and achieving financial independence. By investing in stocks, real estate, or other assets, you can earn a return on your money and build a portfolio that generates passive income.

To start investing, consider working with a financial advisor to create a diversified investment portfolio that aligns with your goals and risk tolerance. You can also use online investment platforms to make investing more accessible and affordable.

3.5 Mindful Spending:

Mindful spending is the practice of being intentional and deliberate about how you spend your money. It involves considering your values and priorities and making purchases that align with them.

To practice mindful spending, start by identifying your values and priorities. Then, when making purchasing decisions, ask yourself if the item or experience aligns with those values. If it does not, consider whether it is worth spending your money on.

3.6 Continuous Learning:

Continuous learning is critical for supporting a wealth mindset because it helps you stay informed about financial trends and opportunities. By staying up to date on the latest news and information, you can make informed decisions about your finances and investments.

To engage in continuous learning, consider reading books, attending workshops or seminars, and following financial blogs or podcasts. You can also work with a financial advisor who can provide personalized advice and guidance.

3.7 Goal Setting:

Goal setting is a powerful tool for achieving financial success. By setting specific, measurable goals, you can create a roadmap for achieving your dreams and aspirations.

To set financial goals, start by identifying your long-term goals, such as retirement or purchasing a home. Then, break those goals down into smaller, achievable milestones and create a plan for reaching them. Track your progress regularly and adjust your plan as necessary.

3.8 Minimizing Debt:

Debt can be a significant obstacle to achieving financial independence. By minimizing your debt, you can free up more of your income to save and invest in your future.

To minimize debt, start by creating a plan for paying off any outstanding debts, such as credit card balances or student loans. Consider using the debt snowball or debt avalanche method to pay off debts quickly and efficiently. Then, focus on avoiding new debts by living within your means and practicing mindful spending.

3.9 Accountability:

Accountability is critical for developing healthy habits and routines that support a wealth mindset. By having someone to hold you accountable and provide support, you can stay motivated and committed to achieving your financial goals.

To find accountability, consider working with a financial advisor or coach who can provide guidance and support as you work towards your goals. You can also join a financial support group or work with a friend or family member who shares similar financial goals.

3.10 Healthy Lifestyle Habits:

Healthy lifestyle habits, such as exercise and proper nutrition, can also support a wealth mindset. By taking care of your physical and mental health, you can improve your overall well-being and increase your productivity and energy levels.

To develop healthy lifestyle habits, start by setting realistic goals for exercise, nutrition, and sleep. Consider joining a gym or fitness class, meal prepping, and creating a sleep routine to support healthy habits.

3.11 Gratitude:

Gratitude is a powerful mindset that can support a wealth mindset by promoting positivity and reducing stress. By practicing gratitude, you can focus on what you have instead of what you lack and cultivate a positive attitude towards money and wealth.

To practice gratitude, start by creating a daily gratitude journal and writing down three things you are grateful for each day. You can also practice gratitude meditation or express gratitude to those around you.

In conclusion, developing healthy habits and routines that support a wealth mindset is essential for achieving financial independence and living the life you want. By incorporating budgeting, saving, investing, mindful spending, continuous learning, goal setting, minimizing debt, accountability, healthy lifestyle habits, and gratitude into your daily routine, you can build a strong foundation for financial success. Remember, developing these habits takes time and effort, but with patience and persistence, you can achieve your financial goals and live the life you want.

Chapter 4

4.1 The Connection Between Physical Health and Financial Success

The connection between physical health and financial success is an important aspect of overall well-being. While it may not be immediately evident, there are several ways in which physical health can impact one's financial situation.

Firstly, physical health directly influences our ability to work and earn income. When we are in good physical shape, we have more energy, focus, and productivity, allowing us to perform better in our jobs. This can lead to career advancements, salary increases, and opportunities for additional income. On the other hand, poor physical health can lead to frequent sick days, reduced productivity, and potential loss of employment or income.

Secondly, maintaining good physical health can help minimize healthcare expenses. Regular exercise, a balanced diet, and preventive measures such as routine check-ups and vaccinations can contribute to a healthier lifestyle, reducing the likelihood of costly medical treatments or chronic health conditions. By prioritizing physical health, individuals can save money on healthcare expenses and allocate those funds towards other financial goals.

Furthermore, physical health impacts our mental well-being, which in turn influences our financial decision-making. When we are physically fit, we often experience reduced stress levels, improved cognitive function, and enhanced emotional resilience. This mental clarity and emotional stability can lead to better financial decision-making, including budgeting, saving, and investing. Conversely, poor physical health can contribute to stress, anxiety, and impaired decision-making, which may result in impulsive or detrimental financial choices.

Additionally, physical health habits often extend to other areas of our lives, including our financial behaviors. Discipline, consistency, and self-control, which are essential for maintaining physical health, can also translate into responsible financial habits. For example, sticking to a fitness routine requires commitment and dedication, qualities that can be applied to budgeting, saving, and avoiding unnecessary debt.

Lastly, physical health can have long-term financial implications, particularly in terms of retirement planning. Taking care of our physical well-being now can help prevent or delay the onset of chronic health conditions that may require costly medical treatments or long-term care in the future. By maintaining good physical health, individuals can potentially reduce healthcare expenses during retirement and have more financial resources to enjoy their later years.

In conclusion, there is a clear connection between physical health and financial success. Prioritizing physical health not only improves our overall well-being and quality of life but also positively impacts our earning potential, healthcare expenses, decision-making abilities, financial behaviors, and long-term financial security. By recognizing and nurturing this connection, individuals can strive for holistic well-being and increase their chances of achieving financial success.

Here are some additional points to consider regarding the connection between physical health and financial success:

4.2 Improved Work Performance:

Good physical health can enhance our cognitive abilities, concentration, and problem-solving skills, leading to increased productivity and better job performance. This can result in professional growth, promotions, and higher income potential.

4.3 Reduced Healthcare Costs:

Engaging in regular physical activity, maintaining a healthy diet, and practicing preventive measures can help prevent or manage chronic health conditions. By minimizing the need for medical treatments and interventions, individuals can save on healthcare costs and allocate those funds towards financial goals.

4.4 Enhanced Energy and Vitality:

Physical fitness and overall well-being can provide us with higher energy levels, mental clarity, and vitality. This can contribute to a more active and fulfilling lifestyle, enabling us to pursue personal interests, hobbies, and even entrepreneurial endeavors that have the potential to generate additional income.

4.5 Positive Relationship with Time and Money:

Being physically healthy often requires discipline, time management, and effective planning. These skills can spill over into other areas of our lives, including our financial management. By developing a disciplined approach to our physical health, we can also adopt similar practices when it comes to budgeting, saving, and investing.

4.6 Increased Self-Confidence:

Taking care of our physical health can boost our self-esteem and self-confidence. This positive self-image can have a ripple effect on various aspects of our lives, including our professional endeavors, negotiation skills, and the ability to seize financial opportunities.

4.7 Prevention of Financial Setbacks:

Poor physical health can lead to unexpected medical emergencies or conditions that require expensive treatments or surgeries. By maintaining good physical health, individuals can reduce the risk of such financial setbacks and have greater peace of mind regarding their financial stability.

4.8 Longevity and Retirement Planning:

Adopting a healthy lifestyle can contribute to a longer and more active life. This, in turn, impacts retirement planning as individuals can enjoy more years of financial independence, travel, and pursuing their passions without the burden of excessive healthcare expenses.

4.9 Positive Influence on Others:

When we prioritize our physical health, we become role models for those around us, including family, friends, and colleagues. By inspiring others to take care of their own health, we contribute to a healthier and more productive community, which can have indirect financial benefits for everyone involved.

In summary, the connection between physical health and financial success is multifaceted and intertwined. By investing in our physical well-being, we can reap numerous financial rewards, including improved work performance, reduced healthcare costs, increased energy and vitality, positive financial habits, enhanced self-confidence, prevention of financial setbacks, better retirement planning, and the ability to positively influence others. By recognizing and leveraging this connection, individuals can create a strong foundation for both their physical and financial well-being.

Chapter 5

5.1 How to Cultivate a Positive Relationship with Food and Exercise

Cultivating a positive relationship with food and exercise is essential for maintaining good physical health, overall well-being, and a balanced approach to life. Here are some key strategies to help foster a healthy and positive mindset towards food and exercise:

5.2 Embrace a Balanced Approach:

Instead of viewing food as the enemy or exercising as a punishment, adopt a balanced perspective. Recognize that food is not just fuel for the body, but also a source of enjoyment and social connection. Similarly, approach exercise as an opportunity to take care of your body and improve your fitness, rather than solely focusing on achieving a certain appearance.

5.3 Practice Mindful Eating:

Pay attention to your body's hunger and fullness cues. Eat slowly and savor each bite, focusing on the taste, texture, and enjoyment of the food. Avoid distractions while eating, such as TV or electronic devices, and be present in the moment. Mindful eating can help you develop a better understanding of your body's needs and promote a healthier relationship with food.

5.4 Honor Your Body's Signals:

Listen to your body and give it what it needs. This means eating when you're hungry, choosing foods that nourish you, and stopping when you're satisfied. Avoid restrictive diets or rigid food rules that can lead to feelings of deprivation and an unhealthy relationship with food.

5.5 Shift the Focus from Weight to Health:

Instead of fixating on the number on the scale, prioritize your overall health and well-being. Focus on nourishing your body with nutritious foods and engaging in physical activities that you enjoy and that make you feel good. By shifting the focus to health, you can cultivate a positive mindset towards food and exercise.

5.6 Find Joy in Movement:

Exercise doesn't have to be a chore. Discover physical activities that you genuinely enjoy and that bring you pleasure. It could be dancing, hiking, swimming, playing a sport, or practicing yoga. By engaging in activities that you find enjoyable, you're more likely to make exercise a regular part of your life and develop a positive association with it.

5.7 Ditch the All-or-Nothing Mentality:

Avoid falling into the trap of all-or-nothing thinking when it comes to food and exercise. Allow yourself flexibility and permission to enjoy treats in moderation without guilt. Similarly, if you miss a workout or have an off day, don't let it derail your entire routine. Embrace the concept of progress, not perfection, and focus on consistency rather than occasional slip-ups.

5.8 Seek Support:

Surround yourself with a supportive community or seek professional help if needed. Share your journey with friends, family, or a support group who can offer encouragement and understanding. Consider working with a registered dietitian or a fitness professional to develop a personalized plan that aligns with your goals and values.

5.9 Practice Self-Compassion:

Be kind to yourself and practice self-compassion throughout your journey. Accept that setbacks and challenges are a natural part of the process. Treat yourself with understanding, patience, and forgiveness, just as you would support a loved one going through a similar experience.

By implementing these strategies, you can develop a positive relationship with food and exercise. Remember that it's a continuous process, and it may take time to undo any negative associations or habits. Be gentle with yourself, celebrate progress, and focus on nurturing a healthy and balanced approach to food, exercise, and overall well-being.

some additional points to further explore the topic of cultivating a positive relationship with food and exercise:

5.10 Practice Intuitive Eating:

Intuitive eating is a mindful approach to eating that focuses on honoring your body's hunger and fullness cues, as well as your own preferences and satisfaction. It encourages you to rely on internal cues rather than external rules or restrictions. By listening to your body and trusting its signals, you can develop a healthier and more sustainable relationship with food.

5.11 Foster a Non-Diet Mindset:

Move away from the dieting mentality and embrace a non-diet approach to food and exercise. Diets often promote restriction, deprivation, and a rigid set of rules, which can lead to an unhealthy relationship with food and contribute to feelings of guilt and shame. Instead, focus on nourishing your body with a variety of foods and engaging in joyful movement.

5.12 Challenge Societal Influences:

Recognize and challenge the societal pressures and messages surrounding food and body image. The media often promotes unrealistic body ideals and encourages restrictive diets. By questioning these messages and embracing body positivity and inclusivity, you can foster a healthier mindset and build a positive relationship with food and exercise.

5.13 Cultivate Self-Care Practices:

Prioritize self-care activities that promote both physical and mental well-being. Engage in activities that help you relax, reduce stress, and recharge. This could include practices such as meditation, yoga, journaling, spending time in nature, or engaging in hobbies that bring you joy. Taking care of your overall well-being can positively impact your relationship with food and exercise.

5.14 Focus on Progress, Not Perfection:

Celebrate small wins and acknowledge your progress along the way. Recognize that every step forward, no matter how small, is a step in the right direction. Avoid comparing yourself to others and instead focus on your personal journey and growth. Remember that it's about creating sustainable habits and a positive mindset, rather than achieving perfection.

5.15 Seek Professional Guidance:

If you're struggling with developing a positive relationship with food and exercise, consider seeking guidance from a registered dietitian, therapist, or counselor who specializes in disordered eating or body image issues. They can provide personalized support, guidance, and strategies tailored to your specific needs.

5.16 Be Mindful of Language and Self-Talk:

Pay attention to the language you use when talking about food and exercise. Avoid labeling foods as "good" or "bad" and instead focus on nourishment and balance. Similarly, be mindful of the way you talk to yourself about your body and fitness goals. Practice positive self-talk and cultivate self-compassion to foster a healthy mindset.

5.17 Embrace Variety and Flexibility:

Embrace a varied and flexible approach to food and exercise. Allow yourself to enjoy a wide range of foods, including those that may be considered indulgent or less nutritious, in moderation. Similarly, explore different forms of physical activity to keep things interesting and maintain your motivation.

5.18 Set Realistic and Sustainable Goals:

When it comes to food and exercise, set realistic and sustainable goals that align with your values and priorities. Avoid setting unrealistic expectations or engaging in extreme behaviors that are difficult to maintain long-term. Instead, focus on creating habits that promote overall health and well-being.

5.19 Reflect and Learn:

Take the time to reflect on your experiences with food and exercise. Pay attention to how certain foods make you feel, both physically and emotionally. Reflect on your relationship with your body and the impact it has on your well-being. Use these insights as opportunities for growth and learning, continuously refining your approach and mindset.

Remember, developing a positive relationship with food and exercise is a journey that requires patience, self-compassion, and consistent effort. By implementing these strategies and fostering a mindful and balanced mindset.

Chapter 6

6.1 The Importance of Rest and Recovery for Productivity and Success

Rest and recovery are often overlooked in our fast-paced, productivity-driven society. Many people believe that success and productivity are solely dependent on working long hours and pushing ourselves to the limit. However, the truth is that rest and recovery are essential components of sustainable productivity and long-term success. In this section, we will explore the importance of rest and recovery, their impact on productivity and success, and practical strategies for incorporating them into our lives.

6.2 Physical and Mental Restoration:

Rest and recovery provide an opportunity for our bodies and minds to heal and recharge. Physically, it allows our muscles to repair and rebuild, reducing the risk of injury and improving overall physical performance. Mentally, it gives our brains a chance to rest and rejuvenate, enhancing cognitive function, focus, and creativity.

6.3 Enhanced Productivity and Efficiency:

Contrary to popular belief, consistently working long hours without breaks or adequate rest does not lead to higher productivity. Research has shown that taking regular breaks and getting sufficient rest actually improves focus, concentration, and problem-solving abilities. It allows us to maintain high levels of performance over an extended period, leading to increased productivity and efficiency.

6.4 Preventing Burnout:

Overworking and neglecting rest and recovery can quickly lead to burnout, a state of physical, mental, and emotional exhaustion. Burnout can have severe consequences on our overall well-being, work performance, and personal relationships. By prioritizing rest and recovery, we can prevent burnout and maintain a healthier work-life balance.

6.5 Mental Health and Emotional Well-being:

Rest and recovery play a crucial role in maintaining good mental health and emotional well-being. Chronic stress and exhaustion can contribute to anxiety, depression, and other mental health issues. Taking time to relax, unwind, and engage in activities that bring us joy and relaxation can significantly improve our mental health, reduce stress levels, and enhance our overall quality of life.

6.6 Creativity and Problem-Solving:

Rest and relaxation stimulate our creativity and enhance our problem-solving abilities. When our minds are constantly engaged in work and tasks, we may find ourselves in a state of mental fatigue, making it challenging to think outside the box or find innovative solutions. Taking breaks, engaging in leisure activities, and allowing our minds to wander can ignite our creative thinking and help us approach challenges from different perspectives.

6.7 Improved Decision-Making:

Rested and rejuvenated individuals are more likely to make better decisions. When we are tired or mentally drained, our cognitive abilities, judgment, and decision-making skills can become compromised. Taking the time to rest and recover allows us to approach decisions with clarity, rationality, and sound judgment.

6.8 Physical Health and Longevity:

Rest and recovery contribute to overall physical health and longevity. Chronic sleep deprivation and a lack of rest can lead to various health issues, including cardiovascular problems, weakened immune function, and increased risk of chronic diseases. Prioritizing restful sleep and incorporating recovery practices, such as relaxation techniques and stress management, support our overall health and well-being.

6.9 Work-Life Balance:

Rest and recovery are vital for maintaining a healthy work-life balance. In a society that often glorifies busyness and constant productivity, it's crucial to establish boundaries and create time for rest, leisure, and personal activities. By prioritizing rest and recovery, we can achieve a more balanced and fulfilling lifestyle, allowing us to excel both professionally and personally.

Practical Strategies for Incorporating Rest and Recovery:

6.10 Prioritize Sleep:

Make quality sleep a priority by establishing consistent sleep patterns, creating a conducive sleep environment, and practicing good sleep hygiene.

6.11 Take Regular Breaks:

Incorporate short breaks throughout your workday to rest, stretch, and recharge. Use techniques like the Pomodoro Technique, where you work for focused intervals followed by short breaks.

6.12 Engage in Relaxation Practices:

Dedicate time each day for relaxation practices such as meditation, deep breathing exercises, mindfulness, or yoga. These practices promote relaxation, reduce stress, and enhance overall well-being.

6.13 Unplug from Technology:

Disconnect from electronic devices, especially before bedtime. Set boundaries to limit screen time and create designated tech-free periods to allow your mind to rest.

6.14 Engage in Leisure Activities:

Make time for activities that bring you joy, such as hobbies, sports, spending time in nature, or engaging in creative pursuits. These activities provide a sense of fulfillment, relaxation, and rejuvenation.

6.15 Practice Mindfulness:

Cultivate present-moment awareness and engage fully in each activity you undertake. This allows you to savor the moment, reduce stress, and improve overall focus and clarity.

6.16 Establish Boundaries:

Learn to say no and set boundaries to protect your time and energy. Prioritize activities that align with your values and goals, and don't overcommit yourself.

6.17 Seek Support:

Reach out to friends, family, or professionals for support and guidance. Discussing your challenges and seeking advice can provide valuable insights and help you navigate the journey of rest and recovery.

In conclusion, rest and recovery are essential components of a balanced and successful life. By acknowledging their importance and incorporating strategies to prioritize rest and recovery, we can enhance our productivity, well-being, and overall success. Remember, rest is not a sign of weakness but rather a strategic investment in our long-term physical, mental, and emotional health. So, let us embrace rest, take care of ourselves, and cultivate a life of productivity, balance, and fulfillment.

Chapter 7

7.1 The Power of Positive Thinking for Your Overall Health and Wealth

The power of positive thinking extends beyond our emotional well-being and has a profound impact on our overall health and wealth. Positive thinking involves adopting an optimistic mindset, focusing on the positive aspects of life, and actively cultivating positive thoughts and beliefs. In this section, we will explore the connection between positive thinking and our health and wealth, and how it can influence our lives in significant ways.

7.2 Improved Physical Health:

Numerous studies have shown a correlation between positive thinking and improved physical health. Positive thinkers tend to have lower levels of stress, reduced risk of chronic diseases, and stronger immune systems. They also exhibit healthier lifestyle habits, such as regular exercise, a balanced diet, and better sleep patterns. Positive thinking can enhance our physical well-being by reducing stress hormones, boosting immune function, and promoting overall vitality.

7.3 Enhanced Mental Health:

Positive thinking plays a crucial role in maintaining good mental health and well-being. It can help reduce symptoms of anxiety and depression, enhance resilience, and improve overall psychological functioning. Positive thinkers tend to have better coping mechanisms, higher self-esteem, and greater emotional well-being. By focusing on positive thoughts and beliefs, we can shift our perspective, reframe challenges, and cultivate a more optimistic outlook on life.

7.4 Increased Resilience:

Positive thinking strengthens our ability to bounce back from setbacks and challenges. When faced with adversity, positive thinkers are more likely to maintain a hopeful attitude, seek solutions, and persevere through difficulties. This resilience allows us to overcome obstacles, adapt to change, and continue moving forward towards our goals. By embracing positive thinking, we can build emotional resilience and navigate life's ups and downs with greater ease.

7.5 Enhanced Problem-Solving Skills:

Positive thinkers approach problems and obstacles with a solution-oriented mindset. They focus on possibilities, alternatives, and creative solutions rather than dwelling on limitations or setbacks. This positive mindset enhances problem-solving skills, encourages innovative thinking, and promotes a proactive approach to overcoming challenges. By adopting positive thinking, we can develop a more resourceful and effective approach to problem-solving in all areas of our lives.

7.6 Increased Confidence and Self-Belief:

Positive thinking nurtures a sense of confidence and self-belief. When we believe in ourselves and our abilities, we are more likely to take risks, pursue opportunities, and reach for higher levels of success. Positive thinkers have a stronger belief in their own capabilities and are willing to step out of their comfort zones to achieve their goals. This self-confidence opens doors to new possibilities and empowers us to take action towards creating wealth and success.

7.7 Improved Relationships and Networking:

Positive thinking enhances our interpersonal relationships and networking abilities. Positive thinkers are more likely to attract and maintain positive and supportive relationships. They radiate positive energy, kindness, and optimism, making them more approachable and likable. Positive thinking also cultivates a mindset of collaboration and cooperation, allowing us to build strong networks and attract opportunities through positive interactions with others.

7.8 Increased Motivation and Goal Achievement:

Positive thinking fuels motivation and propels us towards our goals. When we have a positive mindset, we are more likely to set ambitious goals, believe in our ability to achieve them, and persistently work towards them. Positive thinkers maintain a focus on possibilities, maintain an optimistic outlook, and are driven by a sense of purpose and passion. This motivation and goal-directed behavior are essential for creating wealth and achieving financial success.

7.9 Attraction of Abundance and Opportunities:

Positive thinking aligns our thoughts and beliefs with abundance and prosperity. By cultivating positive thoughts and visualizing success, we create a magnetic force that attracts opportunities, abundance, and wealth into our lives. Positive thinkers embrace an abundance mindset, viewing the world as a place of unlimited possibilities and opportunities. This mindset allows us to tap into the power of manifestation and consciously create the financial success we desire.

In conclusion, the power of positive thinking extends beyond our emotional well-being and has a profound impact on our overall health and wealth. By cultivating a positive mindset, we can experience improved physical health, enhanced mental well-being, increased resilience, better problem-solving skills, increased confidence, improved relationships, heightened motivation, and the attraction of abundance and opportunities. Positive thinking is a transformative tool that empowers us to create the life of health, happiness, and financial success we desire. So, let us embrace positive thinking, cultivate optimism, and unleash the power of positive thoughts and beliefs in all aspects of our lives.

Chapter 8

8.1 How to Cultivate a Sense of Gratitude and Appreciation for Life's Abundance

Cultivating a sense of gratitude and appreciation for life's abundance is a powerful practice that can bring immense joy, fulfillment, and a positive mindset into our lives. It involves recognizing and acknowledging the blessings, opportunities, and abundance that exist around us, even in the smallest of things. Here are some ways to cultivate a sense of gratitude and appreciation:

8.2 Mindful Reflection:

Take time each day to reflect on the things you are grateful for. This can be done through journaling, meditation, or simply pausing to mentally list a few things you appreciate. Reflect on the positive aspects of your life, such as good health, supportive relationships, personal achievements, or the beauty of nature. By intentionally focusing on gratitude, you shift your attention away from what may be lacking and instead recognize the abundance already present.

8.3 Appreciation for the Present Moment:

Practice being fully present in the moment and savoring the experiences you encounter. Whether it's enjoying a delicious meal, spending time with loved ones, or witnessing a beautiful sunset, immerse yourself in the present and appreciate the richness of the experience. By paying attention to the details and finding joy in the present moment, you develop a deeper appreciation for the abundance that surrounds you.

8.4 Counting Blessings:

Create a habit of counting your blessings daily. This can be done mentally or by keeping a gratitude journal. Write down three to five things you are grateful for each day. They can be big or small, significant or seemingly insignificant. By regularly acknowledging and documenting your blessings, you train your mind to focus on the positive aspects of life, fostering a sense of gratitude and appreciation.

8.5 Acts of Kindness:

Engage in acts of kindness and generosity towards others. By giving back, volunteering, or helping those in need, you not only make a positive impact on others' lives but also cultivate a deeper appreciation for the abundance you have. Acts of kindness remind us of our interconnectedness and the blessings we can share with others.

8.6 Shift Perspective:

Train yourself to see challenges and setbacks as opportunities for growth and learning. When faced with obstacles, try to find the lessons or silver linings they may bring. By reframing difficulties in a positive light, you develop resilience and a greater appreciation for the abundance of lessons and growth that life offers.

8.7 Gratitude Rituals:

Incorporate gratitude rituals into your daily routine. This could involve starting or ending each day with a gratitude prayer, meditation, or moment of reflection. It sets a positive tone for the day and allows you to cultivate gratitude as a consistent practice.

8.8 Surround Yourself with Positive Influences:

Surround yourself with people who embody gratitude and positivity. Share your gratitude with others and engage in conversations that uplift and inspire. Being around individuals who appreciate life's abundance reinforces your own sense of gratitude and cultivates a positive mindset.

Here are some additional points to consider when cultivating a sense of gratitude and appreciation for life's abundance:

8.9 Gratitude for Lessons Learned:

Embrace the challenges and failures you've experienced as valuable learning opportunities. Recognize that even during difficult times, there are lessons to be gained and growth to be achieved. Express gratitude for the wisdom and resilience you have developed as a result.

8.10 Gratitude for Relationships:

Cultivate gratitude for the meaningful relationships in your life. Express appreciation for the love, support, and connection you share with family, friends, and colleagues. Recognize the positive impact these relationships have on your well-being and overall sense of abundance.

8.11 Gratitude for Personal Growth:

Reflect on your personal growth journey and express gratitude for the progress you have made. Celebrate your accomplishments, both big and small, and acknowledge the effort and dedication you have put into becoming the best version of yourself.

8.12 Gratitude for Nature's Gifts:

Develop a deeper appreciation for the natural world around you. Take time to notice the beauty of nature, whether it's a vibrant sunset, a blooming flower, or the sound of birds chirping. Connect with the awe-inspiring elements of nature and express gratitude for the abundance of beauty and tranquility it offers.

8.13 Gratitude for Simple Pleasures:

Cultivate gratitude for the simple pleasures in life. It could be enjoying a warm cup of tea, listening to your favorite music, or finding joy in everyday moments. By appreciating these small joys, you elevate your overall sense of gratitude and recognize the abundance in the seemingly ordinary aspects of life.

8.14 Gratitude in Times of Adversity:

Challenge yourself to find gratitude even in the face of adversity. During challenging times, there may still be aspects of your life for which you can be grateful. Focus on the strength, resilience, and support systems that help you navigate difficult situations. Expressing gratitude in challenging times can shift your perspective and bring about a sense of hope and positivity.

8.15 Gratitude as a Daily Practice:

Make gratitude a daily practice. Set aside dedicated time each day to reflect on and express gratitude. It could be in the morning as you start your day or in the evening before bed. Consistency is key in building the habit of gratitude and nurturing a mindset of appreciation.

8.16 Gratitude as a Mindset:

Ultimately, cultivating gratitude and appreciation is about adopting it as a mindset. It involves shifting your perspective to see the abundance and blessings that exist in your life, even during challenging times. Embrace gratitude as a way of perceiving the world and approach each day with a grateful heart.

By practicing gratitude and appreciation for life's abundance, you enhance your overall well-being, cultivate a positive outlook, and attract more positivity and abundance into your life. It is a transformative practice that brings joy, fulfillment, and a deep sense of gratitude for the richness of life's experiences.

Part 7 Complete

Conclusion of "The Wealth Mindset"

In conclusion, this book has explored the concept of cultivating a wealth mindset and its profound impact on personal and financial success. We have delved into the power of thoughts and beliefs, the benefits of adopting a wealth mindset, and the examples of successful individuals who embody this mindset. We have examined the connection between mindset and financial success, as well as the role of goal-setting, positive attitude, and taking action in achieving one's financial goals.

Additionally, we have explored the importance of mindset over money, the significance of taking consistent action, and the strategies for maintaining a positive mindset in the face of challenges. We have also discussed the connection between self-worth and financial success, the role of positive self-talk and visualization, and the importance of goal adjustment and flexibility along the journey.

Furthermore, we have delved into the significance of surrounding oneself with positive influences, strategies for eliminating negative influences, and techniques for developing emotional intelligence and effective communication skills. We have emphasized the importance of financial education, knowledge of money management, and the basics of personal finance, investing, and wealth building.

Moreover, we have explored the common financial mistakes to avoid, the importance of developing a financial plan and strategy, and the connection between physical health and financial success. We have discussed cultivating a positive relationship with food and exercise, the importance of rest and recovery, and the power of positive thinking for overall health and wealth. Additionally, we have explored the cultivation of gratitude and appreciation for life's abundance, as well as the techniques for overcoming fear, anxiety, and setbacks along the way.

Throughout this book, we have provided insights, strategies, and practical tips to help readers develop and nurture a wealth mindset. By adopting these principles and practices, individuals can transform their relationship with money, achieve their financial goals, and experience greater fulfillment and abundance in all aspects of life.

Ultimately, the journey toward a wealth mindset is an ongoing process of personal growth, self-discovery, and intentional action. It requires dedication, perseverance, and a commitment to continuous improvement. By integrating the principles and strategies outlined in this book, readers can embark on a transformative journey that will lead them to greater financial success, personal fulfillment, and a life of abundance.

The End

www.ingramcontent.com/pod-product-compliance
Lightning Source LLC
Chambersburg PA
CBHW060823220526
45466CB00003B/950